Waiting for the Barbarians

Also by Lewis H. Lapham

Fortune's Child
Money and Class in America
Imperial Masquerade
The Wish for Kings
Hotel America

Waiting for the Barbarians

LEWIS H. LAPHAM

VERSO

London • New York

First published by Verso 1997
© Lewis H. Lapham 1997
All rights reserved

Verso
UK: 6 Meard Street, London W1V 3HR
USA: 180 Varick Street, 10th Floor, New York, NY 10014-4606

Verso is the imprint of New Left Books

ISBN 1 85984 882 6

British Library Cataloguing in Publication Data
A catalogue record for this book is available from the British Library

Library of Congress Cataloging-in-Publication Data
A catalog record for this book is available from the Library of Congress

Typeset in Garamond by NorthStar, San Francisco, California
Printed and bound in the USA by R.R. Donnelly & Sons

Contents

Waiting for the Barbarians

What are we waiting for, assembled in the forum?

    The barbarians are due here today.

Why isn't anything happening in the senate?
Why do the senators sit there without legislating?

    Because the barbarians are coming today.
    What laws can the senators make now?
    Once the barbarians are here, they'll do the legislating.

Why did our emperor get up so early,
and why is he sitting at the city's main gate
on his throne, in state, wearing the crown?

    Because the barbarians are coming today
    and the emperor is waiting to receive their leader.
    He has even prepared a scroll to give him,
    replete with titles, with imposing names.

Why have our two consuls and praetors come out today
wearing their embroidered, their scarlet togas?
Why have they put on bracelets with so many amethysts,
and rings sparkling with magnificent emeralds?
Why are they carrying elegant canes
beautifully worked in silver and gold?

    Because the barbarians are coming today
    and things like that dazzle the barbarians.

Why don't our distinguished orators come forward as usual
to make their speeches, say what they have to say?

    Because the barbarians are coming today
    and they're bored by rhetoric and public speaking.

Why this sudden restlessness, this confusion?
(How serious people's faces have become.)
Why are the streets and squares emptying so rapidly,
everyone going home so lost in thought?

    Because night has fallen and the barbarians have not come.
    And some who have just returned from the border say
    there are no barbarians any longer.

And now, what's going to happen to us without barbarians?
They were, those people, a kind of solution.

                      C. P. Cavafy, 1898

Introduction

The essays collected in this book can be read as a set of variations on Cavafy's poem. They describe a state of mind, and although written in response to a series of unrelated events caught up in the current of the news—the bombing in Oklahoma City, Nick Nolte's interpretation of Jefferson in Paris, Senator Robert Dole's farewell address to the United States Senate—they all touch upon the forms of magical thinking that induce our own latter-day consuls and praetors, equipped with embroidered press releases instead of scarlet togas and silver canes, to imagine that somehow they can make good their escape into the land of wish and dream.

All but the last essay, which recapitulates the themes implicit in those that precede it, keep pace with a period in the country's political and economic affairs (April 1995 to September 1997) when the news from Wall Street was nearly always cheerful and the news from Washington nearly always glum. Prices on the New York Stock Exchange moved steadily and reassuringly up; numerous corporate entities of large and majestic size merged with other corporate entities of large and majestic size (Boeing with McDonnell Douglas, the Chase with the Chemical bank, the Disney Company with the ABC television network); in California's Silicon Valley it was said that the high-speed information industries were manufacturing new millionaires at the rate of sixty-four a day; Silvester Stallone bought an island off the coast of New Zealand on the instant that it was first pointed out to him from a touring helicopter; Ted Turner presented $1 billion to the United Nations, saying that the gift was "a spur of the moment thing ... like buying a new car." No day passed without the launching of a thousand yachts.

The broadly smiling sense of ease and amplitude in the country's financial markets failed to improve the popular attitudes toward Washington, and the politicians didn't help matters with their constant blaming of one another for the crimes of cowardice and the sin of pride. No day passed without the launching of a new investigation, by congressional committee or special prosecutor, of the FBI's incompetence, the timidity of the drug and welfare laws, the sunken wreck of President Bill Clinton's morals.

After the excitement of the O. J. Simpson trial, which absorbed most of the attention that the national audience could afford to squander on matters of the public interest during the whole of 1995, the stage managers of the 1996 presidential campaign had trouble drumming up a crowd. Most of the staff people hired to promote candidates Clinton and Dole had so little enthusiasm for the task that among themselves and sometimes in the presence of reporters they referred to their employers as "Death Star" and "The Boy." The summer nominating conventions posted television ratings well below those awarded to reruns of *Seinfeld,* and on election day in November only 50 percent of the eligible voters turned up at the polls.

The low turnout confirmed a trend that has been hard to mistake since the Cold War was declared a wrap in the winter of 1989—the turning away from politics in all its forms and declensions, the loss of interest in (or concern for) what the ancient Romans called the *res publica* and our modern orators wistfully remember as "the public square." The newly ascendant American plutocracy, its ranks widely enlarged and its net worth many times multiplied by its sustained prosperity of the last fifteen years, doesn't care for rhetoric and public speaking. The wisdom in office on most suburban lawns holds that politics is the province of small-time crooks, well-paid lobbyists and deadbeat liberals, that it is the successful businessman acting with perfect selfishness who guarantees the safety of the republic. Soon after President Reagan moved into the White House in the winter of 1981, when gold was selling at $800 an ounce and long before the last goodbye to the evil Soviet empire, the word "public" began to lose its prior associations with a common purpose or a necessary good. Public transportation and the public school, public housing, public health, the public statue and the public park—all were once synonymous with the highest hopes of the American enterprise. Not now. Not under the terms of the Contract with America. These days the mention of anything public brings with it the suggestion of slums, disease, theft, ignorance, sullen foreigners and shoving crowds. The connotations signifying bright and beautiful have been reassigned to the word "private"—private schools and private police, private clubs, private trout streams, private hospitals, private planes.

The founders of the American republic thought it incumbent upon a free and freedom-loving people, especially those among them who owned property, not only to practice but also to honor the arts of government. The inheritors of their political estate prefer to leave what they have come to regard as a tiresome chore to the hired help—the speech writers, the bagmen, the media consultants and the lawyers. They substitute the wonder of money for the work of politics, which encourages them in the hope of miraculous rescue, if not by a horde of late-arriving barbarians then by a newly formed battalion of omniscient microprocessors. Cavafy speaks of a confusion of realms, of metaphors impersonating facts and facts disguised as metaphors; the essays in this book describe a similarly dreaming habit of mind, which at least for the moment, imparts to our American experiment the character of a theme-park republic.

Pax Economica

If some great catastrophe is not announced every morning,
we feel a certain void. "Nothing in the paper today," we sigh.
—PAUL VALÉRY

By the second week in January the number of wars in progress in the world had come up to the round sum of one hundred, Mexico was bankrupt, and I was having trouble avoiding people who wanted to talk about the probable collapse of the international monetary system, or the imminent destruction of both the ozone layer and the South Atlantic Ocean. Maybe it had something to do with the weather, but I was coming across so many bearers of bad news that I gladly agreed to attend an exhibition of the late Buckminster Fuller's "World Game" in New Haven, Connecticut, and, by the same day's mail, accepted an invitation to hear Boutros Boutros-Ghali, the secretary general of the United Nations, speak to the Council on Foreign Relations in New York City about the geopolitical design of the next century.

Fuller I remembered as an amateur prophet, a dreaming and enthusiastic man always looking for ways out of the prison of the status quo; Boutros-Ghali I knew to be a subtle Egyptian, accustomed to concealing even the most appalling calamities under the rugs of diplomatic euphemism; and I figured that either the game or the speech might provide some sort of counterpoint to the premonitions of disaster. I was proved wrong, but not for reasons that I could have anticipated.

The performance of the "World Game," which was the first of the two

7

events, took place on the afternoon of January 27 in the ballroom of the New Haven Lawn Club. Similar in its theory and objectives to Monopoly, but played without dice by two hundred people standing on a map roughly the size of a basketball court, it turned out to be best understood as a sermon meant to remind the participants that civilizations perish and money doesn't grow on trees. The map—Fuller's visualization of the globe, not the familiar Mercator projection—travels around the country in the custody of the facilitators and referees from the World Game Institute in Philadelphia, who also supply the necessary briefing books, slides, lesson plans, and paper hats. Over the last twenty years, in university gyms and corporate conference halls everywhere in the country, they have handed out countless sheets of instructions to concerned members of Congress, suspicious business executives, alarmed biophysicists, and bewildered schoolchildren. At the Lawn Club they stretched the map across the full length of the ballroom floor and arranged two hundred graduate students from the Yale School of Management as a set of pawns on a geoeconomic game board.

An early afternoon sun filled the tall French windows with brilliant light, and the students, clutching the mimeographed forms that told their fortunes for the next four hours, sat or slouched against the walls while the head facilitator, a man wearing his hair in a ponytail who looked like he once might have played drums for the Jefferson Airplane, stood under the chandelier in the center of the room—i.e., slightly south and west of the Aral Sea—and explained the rules. Each of the first one hundred students represented 1 percent of the world's population (i.e., 58 million human beings), and at the facilitator's direction they took their places on the map in one of the ten regions (Southeast Asia, North America, Europe, the Indian subcontinent, the Middle East, etc.) assumed to possess a coherent cultural and economic identity. Eighteen students, most of them dressed in soft sweaters and jeans, crowded onto the Indian subcontinent, and seven students stood a good deal more comfortably on North America. The players in each region began the game with an allowance of natural and material resources (energy, food, money, manufactured goods) consistent with the percentages published in the *United Nations Statistical Yearbook* and expressed as symbolic tokens (toy airplanes, candies, plastic fruit) that could be exchanged for other tokens, for bank credit, or, in the best of all possible circumstances, for the slips of blue paper denominated as "certificates of well-being." Once the broad mass of humanity had been settled on the map, the

facilitators divided the remaining hundred students into small sections
representing the agencies of international commerce and goodwill—the
United Nations, multinational energy and food corporations, UNESCO,
the World Bank, the news media. In place of trade goods, the cartels
received large sums of cash, and the benevolent organizations received
the power to levy taxes, impose fines, and enforce laws regulating the
pollution of rivers, the despoiling of forests, and the murder of Cambo-
dians.

The overcrowding on the Asian landmass at the east end of the ballroom made the point about the imbalance between the rich and poor
nations of the earth, but nothing in the rules or on the map took account
of any of the world's sorrows that couldn't be defined as a function of
money. The briefing books assumed the existence of a Pax Economica
arrived at by always rational human beings trading with one another in
always orderly capital and commodity markets, and none of the statistical lists introduced the element of politics or raised the unhappy questions about mankind's inveterate pride, stupidity, and fear.

It needed the better part of an hour to move all the players into
position, to make sure that everybody had enough pencils and was wearing the correct paper hat. Before the referees set the game in motion I
noticed the man with the ponytail over against the French windows,
nodding in a conspiratorial way toward the densely populated southern
latitudes and offering, sotto voce, a last word of advice to the students
wearing the emblems of the food and energy cartels.

"Remember," he said, "those people are desperate."

Left briefly to their first instincts during the early stages of the game,
a few of the more literal-minded students, who apparently had been
reading history instead of management theory, ignored the instructions
about achieving "sustainable agriculture," "racial harmony," or "the con-
vergence of incomes" and chose instead to pursue the simple, old-fash-
ioned pleasures of economic imperialism. Their purposes would have
been well understood by Boris Yeltsin and Saddam Hussein, as well as by
the Chase Manhattan Bank and the General Motors Corporation, but
they failed to persuade a bearded young man wearing dark glasses, seated
as impassively as a stone Buddha on the Malabar Coast, fending off bank
loans as well as bribes. He said that he had no interest in Japanese trade
deals, no matter how lucrative or seemingly benevolent, and that if it
were left up to him, he would as soon see Tokyo sink into the Pacific
Ocean as trade one tusk of ivory from one innocent and unsuspecting

elephant for all the high-definition television screens in Yokohama.

After about half an hour the facilitators interrupted the game for a situation report and a further clarification of the rules. The students playing the parts of media correspondents had been wandering among the continents in search of news, and four or five of them took turns reading their notes into a handheld microphone. Without exception they had a natural bent for the facile phrase, and it was clear that they believed everything they had been told.

"India is super-nice."

"Africa has stolen North America's oil."

"Europe has an attitude problem."

A few students had been caught stealing toy airplanes and plastic oranges, and a referee explained that outright robbery, a practice to which he referred as "spontaneous resource allocation," didn't quite fit either the spirit or the specifications of the game. He hoped that the participants would bear in mind Fuller's injunction to increase one's wealth by peaceful means (trade or production or purchase) and to rely on the blessing of human intelligence rather than trust to the bluster of gunboats.

The subsequent rounds of play brought forth models of Utopia worthy of Sir Thomas More. Even though the facilitators complicated matters by updating the bulletins of approaching doom—the always heavier burden of the world's population, the increasing number of countries threatened by starvation, higher prices for oil, the spread of disease—the students, who apparently had missed the morning's headlines (about Mexico's debt, refugees wandering south in Rwanda, civil war in Chechnya), bid up the market in miracles. The paper hats representing the once-upon-a-time Soviet Union paid $15 billion to the paper hats representing the United Nations, and by so doing permanently removed from within their borders all traces of ethnic conflict. Africa rid itself of AIDS and female circumcision; political oppression vanished from the plains of China; and throughout the whole of Latin America the ruling oligarchs distributed their land, their cattle, and their coffee trees to grateful and deserving peasants. The ballroom filled with the shouting of prices bid and asked for Paradise regained, and from time to time above the din of voices the excited cry of "Media man! Media man!" preceded the announcement of yet another forest rescued, another river saved.

But what was truly wonderful about the game was the news that everybody won. Four hours after the first tentative exchanges of toy airplanes and plastic oranges, the facilitators stopped trading for the afternoon and asked for summary statements. Once again the microphone was passed around the room, and one by one the delegations rose to make their reports. The energy cartel had obtained a 50 percent profit on its investments; the U.N. not only solved nine of the ten global problems to which it had been assigned but also had accumulated an immense reserve of surplus cash; the commercial banks held mortgages on the entire world; and the spokesman for the transnational food cartel was so overwhelmed by its financial success that he could barely speak. "I'm not sure I'm supposed to say this," he said, "but we're rich. No, not just rich, but really, really rich." Offered partly as a modest boast and partly as a sheepish confession, the statement was greeted with spontaneous cheering.

Five days later in New York, listening to Boutros-Ghali address two hundred senior members of the American corporate establishment in a Manhattan drawing room, I wondered why he wasn't wearing his paper hat. The setting was a good deal more formal—sober gentlemen in dark suits taking discreet notes with gold pencils, a faultlessly tailored diplomat in place of the man with the ponytail, no game cards, no slide projections, no cries of "Media man!"—but the similarities between the two occasions were more striking than the differences. Like the business-school students in New Haven, the prosperous executives whom the students hoped to become conceived the future as a product sold for money, the peace of nations as an equation in advanced economics.

Introduced by David Rockefeller as a man of great wisdom and unparalleled insight into the hearts of men, Boutros-Ghali talked about the ways and means of defending the castles of wealth against the onslaught of the world mob. The task was becoming an increasingly troublesome one, and the U.N. didn't have enough money or troops (not nearly enough money or troops) to keep up with the demand for early rescues and timely interventions. He mentioned the 70,000 soldiers presently under the U.N. command, thinly distributed around the world in sixteen different peacekeeping operations and running up expenses at the rate of $3.6 billion per annum, and pointed out that with annual dues payments of only $1.8 billion from its member states, the U.N. couldn't very well maintain a decent standard of global decorum.

Hearing Boutros-Ghali speak, I thought of the manager of a once prosperous golf resort or grand hotel making his report to the grounds committee, explaining that decent help was expensive and hard to find, and that the parking of tanks on the sixteenth fairway tended to spoil the grass. If the U.N. had a standing army, it could send a thousand paratroopers to places like Kigali before the trouble started, and thus (for the relatively modest price of $50 million) prevent the outbreaks of genocide that later might cost as much as $500 million to repair. As the loyal servant of the international community, he was bound to carry out the instructions of the U.N. Security Council, but what was he to do if the Security Council had no instructions, if the troops went home because they hadn't been paid, and if the member states didn't know what it was that they wanted or expected of the U.N.? Always he was finding himself "back at square one," each new crisis requiring a new set of responses, and no lessons ever being learned that could be applied on a different continent or carried forward into the next year. Like any other good club steward he knew how to make do under reduced circumstances, and if what the members intended was that the U.N. show up on state occasions disguised as a fig leaf or a scapegoat, he was happy to oblige, but then he couldn't be held responsible for the condition of the putting greens or the corpses found every morning on the beach. The ladies and gentlemen in the drawing room listened to the secretary general's remarks with attentive and solemn respect, and at the end, after a few ornamental questions that didn't dwell on the $1 billion in unpaid dues owed to the U.N. by the United States, they expressed their appreciation with a murmur of polite applause.

What was missing from the drawing-room discussion, just as it had been missing from the board game played in the ballroom, was the sense that the new set of circumstances forced on the world by the events of the last fifty years might require a new set of blueprints from which to construct an intelligible and realistic foreign policy. At the end of the Second World War in the summer of 1945, the rest of the world was mostly in ruins, and the rulers of the American state found it easy enough to believe that they could buy the world's friendship for the price of a defense treaty, a bar of chocolate, a carton of cigarettes, or a shipment of steel. The presumption is one that events sooner or later have a way of proving abruptly wrong, but it was also one that we had good reason to dress up in the monumental sculptures of ageless wisdom and certain truth. Men of broad understanding and generous impulse, several of them members of the Council on Foreign Relations, organized the Marshall Plan as well as the innumerable instruments of public policy and private charity through which the United States distributed grain, bank credit, technology, and lofty sentiment to the less-favored nations of the earth. Setting aside as irrelevant the objection that the United States hoped to make the world safe not only for democracy but also for the multinational corporations traded on the New York Stock Exchange, the notion of a Pax Economica served to answer all the questions at hand. Fifty years later, the expressions of American goodwill have begun to take on the character of ransom payments.

Our generosity achieved its most impressive effects among those nations previously endowed with a tradition of wealth, trade, industry, and education. Western Europe prospered, and so did Japan. But the countries that in 1945 were poor, agricultural, and illiterate remain as they were before the advent of American idealism—still illiterate and poor, still dependent on foreign bank loans, and the distinction between the havens and the have-nots begins to take on the aspect of a terrible permanence. The world's misery multiplies at an exponential rate, and among people with little to hope for and nowhere to go, the choice between peace and war presents itself as a tactical rather than a moral question. If the United States still had enough money to fill all the empty suitcases likely to be brought to Washington in the next twenty years, maybe we could continue to afford the pleasant abstractions customary among people rich enough to make of their wealth a substitute for courage or thought. Most Americans, like the students in the ballroom and their senior officers in the drawing room, find themselves morally disarmed when confronted by the visible suffering of people who haven't much chance of life, let alone liberty and the pursuit of happiness.

Lacking the cash to pay the ransoms, what do we offer in its place? How do we preserve the fiction of our innocence? On what ethical ground do we justify our prosperity and defend what remains of our freedom? The questions are moral ones and therefore unpleasant, and for the time being it is easier to put them off until next Tuesday, or postpone them to the next presidential election, or reserve them for a really impressive occasion—a war between Israel and Iran, say, or the firebombing of Moscow.

On the morning after Boutros-Ghali's speech, the signs and portents in the newspapers were no less ominous than they had been in mid

January—at least half the states within the old Soviet Union threatening
to secede from the new Russian Federation, an earthquake in Japan and
a new war in Peru, the U.N. estimating the annual profits of the international crime syndicates at $750 billion—but I could take comfort in
the thought that they could be safely ignored, at least for the time being,
and that with a little luck and a clever advertising campaign, the dealers
in miracles and redemptions could look forward to an era of unparalleled
prosperity.

April 1995

Washington Rain Dance

A party which is not afraid of letting culture,
business, and welfare go to ruin completely can be
omnipotent for a while.
—JAKOB BURCKHARDT

When the Senate in late January took up the question of a balanced-budget amendment I had thought that the conversation was going to be about money. At the end of the debate in early March, I understood that the senators, or at least the Republicans among them, had been talking about sin. The entire sum of their argument rested on confessions to their lack of judgment and character, and one by one over a period of thirty days and thirty nights they came forward into the well of the Senate to beg forgiveness for the weaknesses of the flesh. What they were saying, in effect, was that they possessed neither the courage nor the will to limit their expenditures, that left to their own devices, or set free on their own recognizance, they would squander what little remained of the country's fortune. Not intentionally, of course, and not because they didn't know any better but because they were politicians, and politicians, by definition spendthrift, can't be trusted with the handling of other people's money. Thus their need, "the very desperate need, Mr. Chairman," for a cage. In the prison of the law, within a Twenty-eighth Amendment as binding as the First maybe they would be safe—safe from themselves, safe from the Devil and John Maynard Keynes, safe from the abyss of debt. C-SPAN broadcast the proceedings throughout the month of February, and as I

15

watched the Republican senators take their contrite turns at the ros-
trum, I wondered what had become of the gospel of self-reliance. What
had they done with their albums of golden platitudes about "personal
responsibility"? With their inscribed copies of William Bennett's *Book of
Virtues*? How and when had they become the play-things of blind destiny
and the victims of cruel circumstance?

On the campaign hustings last fall they had gone to no small trouble
to present a contrary impression. Posing for the television cameras in the
attitudes of firm resolve, they showed themselves off as the kind of
people who welcomed risk and "hard moral choices," who knew what it
meant to meet a payroll or break a horse, who stood on their own feet
and chopped their own wood. When in need of an easy laugh or a
bracing round of applause, they made fun of the shiftless and dependent
poor, and I remembered Phil Gramm, the senator from Texas and already
a declared candidate in next year's presidential election, taking a particularly hard line against both the extravagant distribution of food stamps
("We're the only nation in the world where all our poor people are fat")
and the coddling of old people with expensive medical treatment ("Most
people don't have the luxury of living to be eighty years old, so it's hard
for me to feel sorry for them"). Although not always expressed with
Gramm's belligerent self-righteousness, similar sentiments decorated
the speeches of Senators Hatch, Simpson, and Dole—all of them dis-
mayed by welfare mothers unable to restrain their sexual enthusiasms,
by deadbeat fathers sneaking out of the duty to raise their own children,
by unemployed miscreants in various forms and denominations refusing
to govern their own lives and asking for nothing better than to be cared
for by the state.

And yet here were these same noble Romans, these same nominally
independent sons of the honest American soil, refusing to govern either
themselves or the country, sneaking out of their legislative duties, unable to inhibit their fiscal enthusiasms. The Constitution assigns to
Congress the power of the purse, but the Republican senators didn't
wish to exercise that power (on the ground that it might prove hazard-
ous to their chances for reelection), and so they offered a balanced-
budget amendment as a means of shifting their responsibility to a
mathematical formula and the judgment of the courts.

When the legislation failed to pass, on March 2, by the theatrical
margin of a single vote, Pete Domenici, chairman of the Senate budget
committee, was quick to provide the excuse that satisfied the purposes of

all present. In the absence of a constitutional amendment, he said, "it'll be very difficult to balance the budget." But after so many fine and self-flagellating speeches, certainly nobody could blame the Republicans for the government's financial disorder. Neither were the Democrats at fault (because they belonged to the minority party), and after a month of handsomely staged debate, the winter morality play was brought to a close with the best and happiest of all possible endings: nothing changed, everybody was given the chance to act a hero's part, and nobody was responsible.

If I've been reading the papers correctly, the bulk of the legislation put forward in Congress during the first hundred days of the Republican supremacy aspires to more or less the same benign result. The House of Representatives busied itself all winter with a series of measures restricting the government's authority to act on behalf of such a thing as the common good. Let the corporations do as they please—pillage the environment, falsify their advertising, rig the securities markets—and it is none of the federal government's business to interfere with the will of heaven. Let the several states do as they please with the criminal laws, or the schools, or the money meant for the relief of the poor—and again it is not the responsibility of the federal government to attempt the amelioration of man's inhumanity to man. A bill assigning a line-item budget veto to the President (thus further reducing the congressional power of the purse) was followed by the appointing of a nonpartisan commission to decide which of the nation's military bases must be closed, or reconfigured, or sold for scrap.

By early March it was apparent that Congress hoped to rid itself of as many obligations as it could sell at auction or conveniently refer to somebody else, and I was reminded of a sentence that I had once come across in the writing of Thomas Jefferson: "I have no ambition to govern men; it is a painful and thankless office." The reluctance is nonpartisan, and the safest escape from responsibility (for Democrats as well as Republicans) requires the substitution of the appearance of a thing for the substance of a thing. On the day that the Senate failed to pass the balanced-budget amendment, the *New York Times* obligingly found an expert, a visiting fellow at the Brookings Institution by the name of Charles O. Jones, to make the necessary apologies. "The Senate," he said, "is essentially an institution that can't be led. Leading the unleadable is a tough task."

As an alibi for all occasions, the statement could hardly be improved upon, but it ignored the probability that the Congress never had any intention of balancing the budget. Had Senator Robert Dole, the Republican majority leader, truly wished to force the proposition into law, he could have demanded the acquiescence of Senator Mark Hatfield, who offered to resign his seat as a way of allowing the legislation to pass. Dole declined to exercise the option—for the good and sufficient reason that the Republicans were better served with rhetorical gestures than with an actual shortage of funds. So also in the House of Representatives, Speaker Newt Gingrich can propose violent measures meant to restore the country to its original and blessed state of anarchy, all the while knowing that he can trust the Senate to tamp down the flame of revolution or count upon the President to veto the storming of the palace.

Prior to the Great Depression and World War II the Congress conducted itself in the high-handed manner of a nineteenth-century railroad cartel, fiercely protective of its freedom to act. The New Deal and also construction of the national security state sapped the legislative body of both its independence and its resolve, and by 1950 President Truman could blithely declare a war in Korea without bothering to ask Congress for its opinion, much less its advice and consent. Following the resignation of President Richard Nixon and the loss of the Vietnam War, Congress briefly remembered its prerogatives, and for a few years it threatened to assert its constitutional authority to shape the country's laws. The impulse faded during the Reagan Administration. What was to be gained by possibly injurious argument when it was easier to go along with the fiction of Paradise regained? Eager to collaborate with the lobbyists amending the law to satisfy the rapacious spirit of the age, glad to inflate the debt with money borrowed from the Japanese, the Congress assigned the White House as many emergency powers as might be necessary to govern the country in its permanent absence.

The self-styled revolutionaries now at large on Capitol Hill apparently intend to complete the work of abdication. If they can escape responsibility for the budget (as well as for the condition of the country's rivers, jails, cities, markets, schools, and roads), maybe they can transform themselves into a national ballet company or, even better and probably more in line with technological trends, into a regiment of radio-talk-show guests, free to discuss, solemnly and perhaps forever, precisely those issues (sex and American history, family values, school prayer, and "moral responsibility") about which the federal government can do absolutely nothing.

But if the search for the perfect alibi is as nonpartisan as the hope of hitting the lottery and the all-American quest for true romance, neither is it specific to politicians. Our native genius for dodging blame matches our talent for staging aerobic dance routines, and when confronted with the prospect of a decision—about who sits in the corner office, or where to build the factory, or what name to attach to the product or the heroine—we draw back from the precipice of action and we profess our ardent love of freedom and congratulate one another on our rough-hewn individualism, our scoffing at convention, our rebel's nonconformist heart. If the images protest too much (in the ads for Ralph Lauren's clothes as well as in the commercials selling trucks) possibly it is because we know the story is so seldom true. Encountered in person instead of in the movies, freedom proves a good deal less of a risk-free environment than it appears in its press notices, and when we can't escape responsibility by referring the decision to a computer program or a company policy we bind ourselves with addictive drugs or drift off into the narcotic haze of twenty-four-hour television—never of our own free will, of course, but because we can't help ourselves, because father was a politician or mother left us out in the rain.

Although I've never come across the theorem in a science text, I suspect that the law of the conservation of risk behaves in a manner analogous to the law of the conservation of energy. The risk can be made to move around in time and space, as if it were the ace of diamonds in a game of three-card monte, but it doesn't disappear. The Congress might exempt the corporations from the chore of caring for their customers (or the land and water from which they extract their profits), but then the risk becomes political instead of economic. The limited partners can buy bigger houses in Palm Springs, but they have to hire more bodyguards and travel to Iceland to see a living fish.

Reading the divinations of the future that now appear every three or four days in the popular press as well as the policy journals, I gather that we can look forward to steadily rising degrees of risk in a world unable to suppress its appetite for financial speculation or its passion for civil war. If matters become as bleak as the best-selling prophets say, I expect the congressional corps de ballet to achieve a level of performance unmatched since Nijinksy danced Petruschka, or the immortal Markova astonished Moscow with the tragic beauty of her dying swan.

May 1995

Jefferson on Toast

Westforth Communications
1340 Avenue of the Americas
New York, New York 10019

April 20, 1995

Harold Goldenson
Aurora Pictures
1805 Avenue of the Stars
Century City, California 90067

Dear Harry,

Between acts of the Stoppard play at Lincoln Center on Tuesday night, Susan Stanton said that she had seen you at the Academy Awards and that you wanted to make a movie that said something important about America. "Harry is really serious about this thing," she said. "He wants something big for a summer release, something in time for the elections." She said you were worried about what's gone wrong with the country.

That's a beautiful thought, Harry, and I know you mean it. Except for Spielberg, I can't think of any other producer in the business that has your kind of courage. But Spielberg is a Democrat and a friend of Barbra Streisand's, and it's easy to make movies from the sentimental left. All anybody needs is a conspiracy theory, an endangered species, and a crooked politician who looks like Michael Caine. You know as well as I,

Harry, that it's always been harder for those of us on the right, particularly in Hollywood. But if the news from Washington is even close to the truth, maybe the times have changed and Natalie won't have to go to Paris to wear her furs.

We've known each other for a lot of years, Harry, and as I've told you before (both as a friend and as a screenwriter), you're going to have to start thinking about history. I know you don't like the idea, and more than once I've heard you say that the kids these days don't know the difference between Adolf Hitler and Abraham Lincoln, and that without the kids we've got nothing at the box office. Nada. No points. No distribution deal. No home video. Zip. But there's some great stuff in the old books, and you see what's been playing on the suburban screens—*Rob Roy, The Madness of King George, The Last of the Mohicans, Jefferson in Paris.* Maybe the kids can't spell, but they like the clothes.

I also don't know how else you can get across what I think you're trying to say about where and how the country lost its moral sense. I've heard you talk about the lack of respect for authority, about the imbecile news media and corporate lawyers who look and sound like Kato Kaelin. All good points, Harry, and well worth repeating as often as possible to anybody at the bar at Spago who has the wit to listen, but I think you make Gingrich's mistake about the Sixties. It wasn't the Sixties that wrecked the place. Things went wrong a long time before the Beatles showed up in the Hollywood Bowl and Charles Manson broke into the house in Benedict Canyon.

As I've also told you more than once, the trouble started with the American Revolution. The wrong side won the war, Harry, and it's about time that somebody said so. For two hundred years the British have been taking a very bad rap. They weren't the villains of the piece. Not by any means. You've stayed at Clivedon—two years ago if I remember correctly, during the matches at Wimbledon—and you once had dinner with Larry Olivier. You've met Prince Philip, and so you know what kind of people wrote the Magna Carta and invented constitutional government. People who believed in family values and understood the importance of property. Hearts of oak, Harry, marooned in a godforsaken wilderness in 1765, badgered by ungrateful tinsmiths, fighting for the cause of Western civilization.

If you saw *The Madness of King George,* you'll remember the last scene, when the king has recovered his wits and stands with his wife and sons on the steps of a palace, acknowledging the cheers of his loyal subjects.

"Smile at the people," he says to the Queen and the Prince of Wales. "Wave to them, let them see that we're here." That's why you want to make the movie, Harry, to impart to our own Anglo-Saxon establishment a similar sense of well-being—to recover for the members of the Los Angeles Country Club the lost belief in their own legitimate authority, to teach somebody else besides Michael Jordan how to smile and wave.

I haven't worked out a script, but at this point I'd urge you to think about the purpose of the film and the sensation that it would be bound to make. Why let Oliver Stone take up all the space on the Op-Ed page of the *New York Times*? With the larger points in mind, I've taken the liberty of making a few notes:

1. THE EIGHTEENTH CENTURY

Fairfield County's dream of heaven. Where we would all hope to go if we knew the right travel agent. Look at *Jefferson in Paris* and what do you see? Handsome lawns, lovely buildings, footmen standing behind every chair. The Republican Party in silk. The picture of a world that doesn't worry itself about class privilege and the distance between the rich and the poor. Carriages drive through the rabble in the streets of Paris in 1776, and the ladies and gentlemen on their way to a costume ball or a fireworks display don't feel obliged to wonder whether the horses might be trampling to death an occasional orphan. Even more to the point, it's easy to tell the difference between the superior and inferior classes. The former wear ruffles and brocade and amuse themselves with gossip about the political and sexual scandals of the day. The latter appear in rags, filthy and gap-toothed, shaking their fists and shouting unintelligible obscenities.

The audience experiences a feeling of relief. If so noble an age as that of the eighteenth-century Enlightenment could tolerate without guilt or remorse so lopsided a division of the world's wealth, then why should those of us here in a theater in Westwood fret about the new economic order emerging from the financial chaos of the late twentieth century?

As long ago as 1981 I remember you saying that democracy was an idea whose time had come and gone. You were on your way to Washington for Reagan's inauguration, and we were talking book deals at the Regency Hotel with a New York literary agent who thought that Jimmy Carter was a friend of the common man. "Some of us were born to pick ties on Rodeo Drive," you said then, "and others of us were born to pick lettuce in Salinas." A wonderful line, Harry, and, as always, you were ahead of the polls—ahead of Bill Casey, ahead of Buchanan and Limbaugh, even ahead of Henry Kravis and Martha Stewart.

Think of the *ancien régime* as an advertisement for the great, good American place—like an expensive Virginia suburb, or a well-run golf resort in Scottsdale, Arizona—and you have the beginning of a movie about what was lost to the world at Saratoga in the autumn of 1777. Believe me, Harry, you'll be doing your countrymen a favor. They're rich, but they don't know how to behave. Merchant Ivory have made their production company into a school of manners, and Scorsese attempted the trick in *The Age of Innocence,* but nobody has your brio, Harry, and nobody else can teach Cleveland how to walk on parquet.

2. THE AMERICAN REBELS

Most of them were debtors and tax cheats, and when they weren't smuggling contraband (usually rum but sometimes tea or slaves), they were forever dividing into quarrelsome factions, imagining rights where none existed and complaining about affronts to their dignity. Britain financed the Seven Years' War against the Indians and the French, paying for the defense of New England and granting God knows how much government money to people who thought that Parliament owed them a comfortable living. And what was the response when the crown attempted to reduce the subsidy? Insolence and rebellion. Speeches in Boston's Faneuil Hall as wrongheaded as the editorials in the *New York Times* complaining about the taking away of the welfare soup. Sam Adams was as much of a malcontent as Anthony Lewis or Mary McGrory, as far off the wall as Noam Chomsky, and as badly dressed as William Kunstler.

We would need to be careful with the major figures. If seen at all, they should be seen in passing or in the distance, their wigs slightly askew and their characters just enough at odds with the standard portraits to cast doubt on their objections to the British monarchy. We see in Washington his love of uniforms and portentous silences, a man forever posing for a marble statue; Jefferson talks too much and James Otis drinks; in Lafayette we see the self-importance of somebody like Donald Trump; and in Tom Paine, a stubborn intransigence that finally buried him in a pauper's grave.

The loyal American Tories occupy the foreground of the story, sober and well-to-do merchants who sent to London for their gold-headed canes and to Paris for their wine. People who kept faith with the crown of England—i.e., the original Contract with America. All men of property and sense, Harry, like most everybody you know in Bel-Air, people who saw, all too clearly, what was likely to become of a country given over to the passions of the mob and the theories of Jean-Jacques Rousseau.

Susan said that you wanted a piece of paper before the end of the week, but my notes are in the house at East Hampton, and my memory doesn't serve me as well as it once did. The names of a number of worthy characters nonetheless come more or less readily to mind: Thomas Hutchinson in Boston, who wept on reading the account of Charles I's beheading; Mather Byles, who asked, correctly as it turns out, "Which is better—to be ruled by one tyrant three thousand miles away or by three thousand tyrants not one mile away?"; the Reverend James Maury, of Fredericksburg, Virginia, a principled clergyman and no stranger to the canon of great books, who put his classical education to practical use in the naming of his slaves—Clio, Cato, Ajax, and Cicero.

Hutchinson was the lieutenant governor of the Massachusetts Colony in the 1760s and by all reports a decent and honorable man. During the Stamp Act Riots the Boston mob tore down his house, literally board by board, smashing the windows, splintering the furniture, dragging the contents of the house (plates, books, portraits, children's clothes) into the muddy street. He was a justice of one of the Crown courts, and the next morning he appeared on the bench in borrowed clothes, and with tears in his eyes he made what even the most zealous patriots present recognized as a particularly fine and affecting speech.

Susan also said that you were anxious to find a role for Uma Thurman, so you should look up the life of Elizabeth Loring, who was known to the Boston newspapers in the 1770s as "a brilliant and unprincipled woman," "the flashing blonde," or, more simply, "the Sultana." Shortly after the Battle of Bunker Hill she seduced Sir William Howe, the general in command of the British army, who found her so engaging that he delayed by six months his assault on Philadelphia. By way of a courtesy to the lady's husband, Howe appointed him a commissary of army prisons in Boston. Loring returned the favor by starving to death most of the American prisoners in his care.

If you choose to make the movie, you almost certainly would want to exploit the character of Gouverneur Morris, a New York aristocrat who wrote the Constitution but retained a profound contempt for democratic theory. He later served as the American ambassador in Paris, and remained in that city (the only foreign representative to do so) during the Reign of Terror. A man of courage, intelligence, and resource, Harry, who shared with Talleyrand the affections of the Comtesse de Flahaut (another possibility for Thurman, or maybe Heather Locklear). When Morris was set upon one afternoon in the Rue de Rivoli by an angry mob intent on hanging him from the nearest tree as an Englishman and a spy, he unfastened his wooden leg, waved it above his head, and proclaimed himself an American who had lost a limb fighting for liberty. The speech was as false as the leg. Morris had suffered his misfortune while escaping through a window from the husband of one of his mistresses—an accident the standard texts still attribute to an overturned carriage or a drunken coachman—but the Paris crowd, as poorly informed and as easily gulled as Costner, congratulated him with a round of spontaneous applause.

As I say, I don't have my notes at hand, but if you decide to go forward with the project, it won't be hard to hire sympathetic historians capable of filling in the architecture and the hats.

3. THE PRODUCTION

Exquisitely photographed, at least three hours long, and with a lot of philosophical speeches about how the dream of liberty and equality always ends up with Robespierre and the guillotine or with Napoleon in the Russian snow. You saw the reviews of *Jefferson in Paris,* and I'm sure you noticed the adjectives—"Opulent," "Lavish," "Elegant," "Gorgeously costumed," "First-class." The critics might as well have been describing a Caribbean beach hotel or the menu at Le Cirque. They loved it, Harry, because they had come to see what civilization was supposed to look like. Footmen running with torches in front of the carriages! Gold lace! Montgolfier's balloon in the garden at Versailles! Wigs! People speaking French! My God, Harry, the Enlightenment!

Believe me when I tell you that you can't miss with this idea. The Republican Party over the last ten years (courtesy of its television and radio and multimedia shows) has prepared the modern audience for the happy return to what the American Tories called "Loyalty and Royalty." I don't know who you get to write or direct, but the casting should be as straightforward as possible: the pretty people (Daniel Day-Lewis, Demi

Moore, Redford) as the British aristocracy and the character actors (Randy Quaid, Tommy Lee Jones, Sigourney Weaver, Tarantino) playing the parts of the colonists. In London we see beautiful women posing for Romney and naval officers brilliantly arrived from Lord Nelson's Mediterranean squadron. Philadelphia looks as poor as threadbare Zagreb or Port-au-Prince. You also might want to consider cameo appearances by the leading figures of the age—Mozart at Kew, Casanova talking about the rustic charms of American women, Talleyrand and Benedict Arnold meeting in the inn at Falmouth.

Susan said that if Pete Wilson becomes president you probably will become the next director of the Voice of America. Make this movie the way I know you can, Harry, and you're more likely to become our ambassador to the Court of St. James's.

When I showed these notes to Susan, she was so excited that she wanted to send somebody to Palio for champagne. "Only Harry," she said. "Only Harry has got the courage to do this thing." She thought that you probably could get Edgar Bronfman to put up the studio money if you convinced him that the movie would win a prize at Cannes.

I'm in the country over the weekend. Let me know when you're ready to talk.

As ever,
David

June 1995

Bomb-o-Gram

A country is not only what it does—it is also
what it puts up with, what it tolerates.
— KURT TUCHOLSKY

*D*uring the same week that a truck bomb murdered 167
people in Oklahoma City, Robert S. McNamara published
his recollections of the Vietnam War, and for a period of
several days on the television news shows the once-upon-a-time secretary
of defense kept bobbing up on the screen in the intervals between the
casualty reports from the Alfred P. Murrah Federal Building. The scenes
of gaping ruin or of Timothy J. McVeigh under arrest were intercut with
those of McNamara, at the age of seventy-eight still as helpful and eager
as a new Boy Scout, seated in a clean and well-lighted studio telling
somebody in a clean and well-lighted suit that the war in Vietnam was a
tragic mistake and that it wasn't his fault if so many people had so
unnecessarily died. The sequence repeated itself often enough to bring to
mind a comparison between the two would-be saviors of Western civilization, the one in shackles and the other frequently in tears, who both
construed heavy explosives as figures of speech. McNamara in the summer of 1965 explicitly defined the bombing raids that eventually murdered upwards of two million people north of Saigon as a means of
communication. Bombs were metaphors meant to win the North Viet-
namese to a recognition of America's inevitable victory, and American
planes dropped what came to be known as "bomb-o-grams" on civilian

29

as well as military targets, less for tactical than for rhetorical reasons. By no means unique in his suppositions, McNamara was both the product and the servant of a society that likes to express itself in the grammar of violence, and he was caught up in a dream of power that substituted the databases of a preferred fiction for the texts of common fact. What was real was the image of war that appeared on the flowcharts and computer screens. What was not real was the presence of pain, suffering, mutilation, and death.

A similar form of reasoning apparently preceded the explosion in Oklahoma City on the morning of April 19. According to the FBI, McVeigh and his associates, among them another veteran of the Persian Gulf War named Terry L. Nichols, delivered a bomb-o-gram in a rented truck, turning 4,800 pounds of fuel oil and ammonium nitrate into a press release.[1] Although it wasn't immediately clear what the message said or to whom it was addressed, presumably it was meant to be understood as a criticism of the federal government. McVeigh and Nichols were known to associate with the kind of people who dress up in camouflage uniforms and believe that the Clinton Administration is a synonym for the Third Reich. Nichols had twice attempted to renounce his American citizenship, and McVeigh had been heard to talk at length about how "this country is going to hell in a handbasket." In February 1992, in a letter that he sent to a newspaper in upstate New York, he had set forth a list of opinions (about high taxes, crooked politicians, and the slipping away of "the American dream") not unlike those expressed by the members of the nation's better country clubs, who bang their fists on the bar and want to know what in God's name had gone wrong with the country since Bing Crosby died. McVeigh's language tended toward hyperbole—"Is a civil war imminent? Do we have to shed blood to reform the current system?"—and it was conceivable that he had read some of the material circulated by the Christian Coalition explaining how the decadent liberal news media sell the nation's soul into bondage,

---

1   Remarking on the traditional American use of violence as emphatic statement, Adam Gopnik, writing in *The New Yorker* in early May, put it as follows: "Last week's bombers ... fit all too well into that bloody tradition, and are all too faithful to its code: Stop thinking of the other person as a person and start thinking of him as an occasion—a blank slate on which to inscribe the Thought for the Day."

or how American presidents unwittingly serve "a new order for the human race under the domination of Lucifer."

But whatever it was that McVeigh and his confederates were trying to say about the country's political and spiritual affairs mattered less than the way in which they chose to say it. The politics were in the form of address, not in the points of argument, and five days after the explosion in Oklahoma City, the correspondent known to police as "The Unabomber" entered the conversation with a mail bomb (a small, heavy package wrapped in brown paper) that killed the man who opened it in an office in Sacramento, California. The force of the explosion blew out the door and all the windows in the room, and in an accompanying letter received the same day by the *New York Times,* the author of the bomb, who apparently had been sending similar compositions for seventeen years (murdering three people and severely wounding twenty-two others), offered to cease hostilities in return for a book contract and certain publication of his treatise on the evils of the "worldwide industrial system." Although presumably meant as singular and obvious statements, the April bombings (appended to the executions carried out over the last year of three people working in abortion clinics) posed a series of ambiguous questions. How do we construe the American idea of freedom if we must communicate with one another by bomb-o-gram?

In what now seems like the good old days before the end of the Cold War, it was supposed to be fairly easy to know who and what was American. Americans weren't Communists. Americans were the freest and happiest people ever to walk the earth, generous to a fault, sometimes criminal and often foolish, but always fair and open-minded and on their way to a bright future. Without the operatic stage set of the evil Soviet empire, the familiar truths no longer seem quite so self-evident, and the future has begun to look a good deal less sunny than it appears in the travel advertisements. The unforeseen collapse of the world-encircling Communist conspiracy removed the dark backcloth against which we were accustomed to project the contrasting images of American innocence and goodness of heart, and in the absence of the Russian antagonists on the totalitarian steppe, how do we recognize the protagonist on the freedom-loving prairie? What kind of people do we wish to become, and how do we know an American when we see one? Is it possible to pursue a common purpose without a common history or a standard text?

The short answer to the last question is probably no. Democracy is a difficult art of government, demanding of its citizens high ratios of courage and literacy, and at the moment we lack both the necessary habits of mind and a sphere of common reference. The marvel of post-modern communications—five hundred television channels, CD-ROMs, the Internet—invites each of us to construct a preferred reality, furnished, like McNamara's theory of Vietnam, with the objects of wish and dream. The commonwealth of shared meaning divides into remote worlds of our own invention, receding from one another literally at the speed of light. We need never see or talk to anybody with whom we don't agree, and we can constitute ourselves as our own governments in perpetually virtuous exile. For every benign us, we can nominate a malignant them (ice people, femi-Nazis, FBI agents, etc.); and for every distant they, a blessed and neighboring we.

Reluctant to address the more difficult questions raised in Oklahoma, the major news media were in no hurry to encourage debate or welcome unedited opinions. It was easier and far less disturbing to ascribe the explosion to lunatics—first Muslim fundamentalists and then American extremists in various denominations—people so abnormal that they couldn't be confused with the boy next door. In support of this interpretation, the media hastily arranged introductions to a number of the country's militia outfits—mostly middle-aged men in paramilitary gear standing disconsolately around with assault rifles in Idaho or Montana—as well as some of the more offensive voices on the talk-radio circuit. As proof of the former, the readers of the country's better newspapers met James (Bo) Gritz, a former Green Beret commander in Vietnam and a founder of Almost Heaven, a Christian Covenant Community convinced that white people are the masters of the earth.[2] As an example of the latter, NBC News ran a televised clip of G. Gordon Liddy, a former White House aide to President Richard Nixon, who conducts a program called *Radio Free D.C.* in which he often and offhandedly refers to the government in Washington as a cabal of despotic tyrants bent on enslaving the American people. The clip showed him advising those of

---

2 Asked for commentary on the Oklahoma bombing, Gritz described it as a "Rembrandt—a masterpiece of science and art put together."

his listeners likely to find themselves under sudden assault to avoid shooting the federal agents in the chest because they would be wearing flak jackets. "Head shots," Liddy said. "Head shots."[3] Again the medium was the message. By their very nature the television cameras couldn't help but present the Oklahoma killing as a new attraction displacing the O. J. Simpson trial at the top of the hour on CNN—not because the producers were cynical, or because they searched out subjects resembling the villains in a James Bond movie, but because everybody in the country understands by now the rhetorical devices of television news. The entire narrative could be inferred from the first five minutes of footage from the Murrah Building—the scenes of catastrophe, the obligatory interviews with local officials making the obligatory announcements, the pundits in Washington worrying about what it all means, a new computer graphic meant to hold viewer attention at least until the first commercial break. The standard packaging doesn't allow for any exceptions to the rules, and the sophisticated viewers, knowing that nothing would be said that might slow the sale of the product, remained free to regard the bombing as pure spectacle. A man had set off a bomb, killing 167 people with the force of an explosion big enough to blow a Toyota 130 miles into the sky, attacking the fundamental premise of American democracy (and thus the life and liberty of every citizen in the country), but we could choose to look upon the event as if it were another melancholy postcard from Rwanda or the first network showing of *Die Hard 2*. Perceived as entertainment, the explosion wasn't an assigned civics lesson, and well before the last of the victims suffocated under the weight of broken concrete, the story had begun to lose its audience and market share. No celebrities had been found in the wreck-

---

3 Among the other items of interest, the newspapers printed excerpts from *Hot Talk* on FSFO-AM in San Francisco—a show on which the guests wonder whether American citizens should be paid a bounty for shooting illegal immigrants (or whether President Clinton is the sworn vassal of a "coven of Communist lesbian members of the Trilateral Commission")—as well as a partial transcript of *The Bob Mohan Show* in Phoenix, Arizona, in which the popular host was complaining about a gun control campaign sponsored by Sarah Brady, the wife of President Reagan's former press secretary. "You know, she ought to be put down," Mohan said. "A humane shot at a veterinarian's would be an easy way to do it. Because of all her barking and complaining, she really needs to be put down."

age, and the more exciting drama of the moment was the one about Michael Jordan's happy return to the Chicago Bulls.

Among the few journalists who wondered whether the explosion might have had something to do with the increasingly poisonous atmosphere of the American political debate, none suggested that McVeigh had campaigned for Oliver North or implied a direct connection between four thousand pounds of ammonium nitrate and the bombast of the reactionary Republican right. They pointed out that Timothy McVeigh wasn't as sophisticated as the Washington columnists and politicians who didn't really mean it when they talked about "pagan tyrants" and "jackbooted thugs," and that maybe his bomb could be understood as a work in mixed media—a crude metaphor made in a basement or a garage instead of a recording studio or a policy institute, less amusing and more literal-minded than the toy anarchism of Bob Mohan or the feckless clowning of Rush Limbaugh, but constructed with the same ideological materials.[4]

The point was well taken, but any and all speculations along such lines were immediately condemned by the prominent news media as "shameless," "transparently self-serving," "plain malicious," "absurd." George Will, the conservative newspaper columnist who also serves as the embodiment of the received wisdom on *This Week with David Brinkley,* codified what promptly became the official as well as the majority opinion. Writing in the *Washington Post* and mustering an impressive roster of historical references (John Brown, Ralph Waldo Emerson, William Butler Yeats, and the Whiskey Rebellion of 1794), Will assured his readers that the "attempt to locate in society's political discourse the cause of a lunatic's action is … contemptible." Similar tones of voice characterized the response of the major Washington news organizations to readings of the Oklahoma City text that didn't agree with their own. The little world within the Beltway is as self-referential as the

---

4 Robert Wright, in *The New Republic:* "Well, certainly it's possible that nationally broadcast statements about an 'enemy' executive branch bent on controlling us could have a decisive and unfortunate influence on a right-wing libertarian paramilitary drifter who already suspects that federal authorities have planted a microchip in his buttocks." E. J. Dionne, in the *Washington Post:* "The country will do itself no favors if it evades a serious discussion of the political meaning of this evil act. It was, finally, motivated by a brand of politics not as detached from the mainstream as we'd like to think."

little worlds within the talk-show nation, and official Washington declines to accept messages unsuitable to an appearance on *Nightline* or a drop-in at a Georgetown cocktail party. The capital is a city of words, but words understood as objects and tokens of power, words as ends in themselves (like fireworks or marble fountains or truck bombs), meant for display and not as expressions of thought. On the Friday after the bombing, two respondents telephoned National Public Radio's *Talk of the Nation* to express inadmissible views, and both of them were quickly silenced by anchors Neal Conan and Nina Totenberg.

CONAN: Let's go to the phones now. Tom, you're on the line in Oakland, California.
TOM: ... We have militia recruiting heavily in Oakland and the San Francisco Bay Area, and actually I run into them because we have shared problems with the authorities in that we're abused by the local government and by the federal government. ... We would be the "Food Not Bombs"—we feed the homeless and were violently attacked by the authorities. I have no respect for the government and I'm a pacifist, and I'm against bombing. I can understand the idea that people would be opposed to the United States government, and I'd like people to reflect on the fact ... that there were in Iraq, there were Oklahoma Federal Building–type bombings that happened every minute all day long. ...
CONAN: Tom! Tom! Tom! Tom! Tom!
(As caller's voice is fading out, we hear him say "and in East Timor" and then NPR cuts caller off entirely.)
CONAN: Good-bye, Tom. Thank you very much. Let's now go to Nick in Charles Town, West Virginia.
NICK: ... I have no sympathy whatsoever for the heinous perpetrators. ... It really gives us an opportunity as a nation to see that the real threats to national security in this country are internal, primarily, and only secondarily and maybe tertiarily external. And the way I would put it is if you look at what's called the quote unquote mainstream political debate in this country, it's become perfectly okay—the coverage loves people like Newt Gingrich and Dornan, and Rush Limbaugh has become a superstar, and it's clear from their rhetoric, from their propaganda ...
TOTENBERG (interrupting): Now you don't really wanna say that. You don't really wanna stick Rush Limbaugh with the bombing, do you?
NICK: No. Let me put it this way: the whole political debate has been put so far to the right that it's understandable that if you tell enough people that the government is the focus of evil and that everything wrong in this country is due to the federal government, and you portray the President as

some kind of a satanic figure who murders people, and, you know ...
CONAN: I'm not sure that any of the people you've identified have talked
about the President as a satanic figure or that this has to do with the
political debate in this country. We're going to have to take a short break ...

President Clinton didn't have much better luck with the Washington
press than Tom in Oakland or Nick in Charles Town. The bodies of the
dead were still being carried out of the rubble in Oklahoma City when
he told an audience of college teachers in Minnesota that the "purveyors
of hatred and division" on some of the nation's radio shows seemed
intent on keeping "some people as paranoid as possible and the rest of us
all torn up and upset with each other." Not unreasonably, he thought the
angry rhetoric harmful to the hope of democratic government—not
because it was angry but because it was made of lies—and of the more
splenetic broadcasters he said, "When they talk of hatred, we must stand
against them. When they talk of violence, we must stand against them."

The President was trying to say that words matter and that sometimes ideas have consequences, but his remarks incited the apologists for
the Republican right to a fury of partisan interpretation. In line with the
general muttering about "the Democrats" changing the currency of human tragedy into the base coin of political insult, Senator Phil Gramm,
the Texas Republican and presidential candidate, all but threatened the
President with a libel action. Newt Gingrich, the speaker of the House
of Representatives, said that it was "grotesque" to imply even a rumor of
a connection between forthright political speech and hateful crime,
"grotesque and offensive" to associate "legitimate questions about the
size and scope of the federal government" with the kind of people who
dress up in camouflage uniforms or referred to "tinhorn bureaucrats" and
federal "Gestapo agents." The conservative majority in the mainstream
press (the *Wall Street Journal, Time* magazine, the columnists William F.
Buckley and William Safire, etc.) cried up the same line of trembling
indignation and vehement denial. The collective sophistry ignored the
Republican campaign rhetoric in last year's elections—for example,
Gingrich attributing the drowning of two small children in a South
Carolina lake to the brutality of a liberal news media—as well as the
Wall Street Journal's fondness for extreme statement—editorials promoting the rumor of Vince Foster's murder or condemning "magazines pub-
lished by thirtysomething women in New York" for leading innocent
midwestern girls into prostitution on Eighth Avenue—and Senator

Jesse Helms, chairman of the Senate Foreign Relations Committee, advising President Clinton last November not to visit North Carolina military outposts unless he was prepared to entertain the risk of assassination.

The denials failed as argument, but they served to reduce the threat of large and disturbing questions—the ones about the prospects of democratic government—to smaller and more trivial subtexts that could be fitted to the rules of the Washington board game and controlled by the mechanics of political spin.[5] What wasn't being said, either in Congress or on the television news, was that the spirit of liberty is never far from anarchy, and that after a while, when the words no longer mean anything, it occurs to people without invitations to *Nightline* that maybe Ted Koppel will listen to a bomb.

Clearly alarmed by so distinct a possibility, the Senate judiciary committee on April 27, eight days after the explosion in Oklahoma, opened hearings on hurriedly redrafted legislation meant to protect the country from outbreaks of terrorism. The bill provided the Justice and Treasury Departments with enlarged powers to keep track of any and all citizens deemed suspicious, and as I watched the C-SPAN broadcast of the testimony, I was struck by the willingness of almost everybody in the room—the senators as eagerly as the witnesses—to exchange their civil liberties for an illusory state of perfect security. They seemed to think that democracy was just a fancy word for corporate capitalism, and that the society would be a lot better off if it stopped its futile and unremunerative dithering about constitutional rights. Why humor people, especially poor people, by listening to their idiotic theories of social justice? In support of McVeigh's dark melodrama about the country "going to hell in a handbasket" (a fiction only slightly different from McVeigh's or from the ones en vogue in places like Palm Springs), all present sought to magnify the threat pressing upon the United States from every quarter of the compass—"domestic fanatics and foreign ideologues,"

---

5 On a television program in late April, I said something to this effect to two Washington correspondents, and I was at once suspected of maligning Bob Dole and the American flag, of imagining a direct and conspiratorial chain of command between Newt Gingrich and a band of paramilitary units wandering with assault rifles through the Dakota Badlands. I hadn't said anything of the kind, but then neither had President Clinton or Tom in Oakland.

neo-Nazis, anti-Semites, members of the Ku Klux Klan, terrorists armed with nuclear or biological weapons backing up their rented trucks to the gates of once-safe suburbs, drifting through the passes in the Rocky Mountains as silently as the Indian tribes that once descended on the luckless General Custer. Louis Freeh, the director of the FBI, recommended supervision of any groups "advocating social or political change," and several witnesses spoke of "open warfare" looming on the horizon of the millennium. And most of them endorsed the principle of "preventive intelligence" and strongly urged a "sustained strategic approach" heavily buttressed by larger sums of money and broader permission to seize bank records and affix wiretaps. The members of the judiciary committee listened to the testimony like children listening to a fairy tale, smiling and nodding at the mention of tagging explosives and decriminalizing chemicals, glad to know that here at last maybe they had found an enemy to take the place of the Russian apparition in the alien snow. Like road-show magicians doing tricks with colored scarves, the witnesses filled the hearing room with the fears that the senators had come to behold, and again I was reminded of distant worlds and sound-proof rooms, of the paranoid romances broadcast to the talk-show nation and drifting like wood smoke through the militia camps in Idaho, of how easily the systems of postmodern communication make possible the retreat into the sanctuaries of the self.

July 1995

Elfland

Technology is the knack of so arranging
the world that we do not experience it.
— MAX FRISCH

When the Speaker of the House of Representatives pub-
lishes a book purporting to set forth his theories of law
and government (as well as his notions of time past and
time future), I figure that anybody who edits a magazine—or writes
about politics, or wonders what might happen next week in Washington—is obliged to read what the man has to say. Last summer Newt
Gingrich published such a book under the title *To Renew America,* and
over the Fourth of July weekend I read enough of it to know that it
couldn't be construed in the traditional sense—that is, in what the
Speaker undoubtedly would scorn as the pre-postindustrial, liberal elit-
ist, countercultural sense of the word "book." It looked like a book, and
the words were in English, but on or about page 12 I understood that it
was meant to be received either as a sacred totem or as some sort of
ingenious electronic device. By the time I reached page 29 (Chapter
Three, "Reasserting and Renewing American Civilization") I began to
look for the cleverly hidden plug that attached the book to a computer
screen or the concealed switch that turned it into a toaster or a fan, and
at page 177 (Chapter Eighteen, "Ending the Drug Trade and Saving the
Children") I performed the same set of experiments that I routinely
bring to the instructions accompanying large or complicated Japanese
toys:

1. Read the sentences from right to left.
2. Read upward from the bottom of the page.
3. Place the first four pages under infrared light.
4. Place the last four pages in warm water.

Nothing worked. I thought of looking through the Yellow Pages for a mechanic, but I didn't know whether I needed somebody who fixed air conditioners or locks, and I remembered that on the Fourth of July even tow trucks are hard to find. It's conceivable, of course, that the book is neither religious artifact nor household appliance, but if Gingrich intended it as a work of history, then what is the reader to make of statements on the order of the following?

> From the arrival of English-speaking colonists from 1607 until 1965, there was one continuous [American] civilization built around a set of commonly accepted legal and cultural principles.

> The world is rapidly becoming a place of serious and intense economic competition.

> Every night on the local news, you and I watch the welfare state undermining our society.

> Look at how rapidly Nazi Germany and Imperial Japan changed from previous generations—and how quickly these malignant cultures were replaced by American models of the rule of law, free speech, and democracy once the war ended.

> One of the most absurd of modern practices is the "war between men and women"—as if God didn't make us both male and female, as if both were not necessary for the propagation of the species.

The voice is digital, grinning, and prerecorded, a theme-park voice not unlike those of Davy Crockett and Robert E. Lee standing watch over the bear paws and Civil War uniforms at Epcot Center. Although Gingrich likes to present himself as a historian, he isn't interested in complicated stories or the ambiguity of human motive and experience. He is a dealer in amulets and good-luck charms, and his text might as well have been assembled by one of the Walt Disney Company's imagineers.

What was striking about the book was its resemblance to the cargo cults that some South Sea islanders constructed prior to the Second World War from the fragments of industrial civilization (copper wires, motors, tin cans, rubber tires) washed ashore from European ships. Gingrich does something similar with his sequences of historical anecdote and quasi-scientific theory. He knows that somewhere over the horizon on the vast ocean of thought, a race of more highly evolved imagineers (physicists, poets, microbiologists, cyberneticians, genuine historians) sail to and fro in vessels of inconceivable power and speed. Some of their names have drifted onto the postmodern beach with the wreckage of the classical literary tradition, and these Gingrich collects as if they were magical shells or stones. Stringing them together into long strands of patriotic but unintelligible sound—George Washington, Information Age, Ray Kroc, Third Wave, Valley Forge, Norman Rockwell, telecommuting, Rush Limbaugh, Tom Edison, Thomas Jefferson, Bill Gates, Apollo 13, Admiral Byrd—he composes a high-speed aluminum om, which, if said very rapidly in unison every morning in the hour before sunrise by every man, woman, and child in America, presumably will put to flight the evil spirit of moral decay, guarantee the profits of important business corporations, make safe the streets of Detroit, restore the glory of the American promise, and assure the nation's happy return to Colonial Williamsburg or Pioneer Village.

I'm sure that *To Renew America* will sell a great many copies, but Gingrich's Magic Kingdom is of as little intrinsic interest as Disney's. Made of the same kind of dreamlike images that float to the surface of MTV, the book conforms to the spirit of an age that delights in its miraculous technologies (whether in the form of cellular phones or herbs thrice blessed by Pocahontas) and assigns the powers once thought to belong to Wotan or Crazy Horse to the kindly elves at Microsoft who spin the golden threads of fiber optics and mine the jewels of silicon. Gingrich shapes his sales pitch to the specifications of the electronic media rather than to those of the written word, and his success (both as author and politician) speaks to the credulousness of an audience eager to substitute legend for history, prophecy for politics, certainty for doubt.

We live in an age no longer possessed of what Neil Postman in *The End of Education* (another new book published last summer, but one meant to be read instead of polished) describes as a "comprehensive narrative" about what the world is like and how and why it came to be that way. Long ago in the torchlight of the Christian past we could explain our ends and our beginnings with reference to the word or glory of God and then, for a few hundred years in the ages of science and reason, with Newton's mechanics or the encyclopedias compiled by the

philosophers of the Enlightenment. But at the end of a century as famous for its mass murders as its Nobel Prizes, we wonder what happened to the world once governed by the telling of a sovereign tale. Like
barbarians putting on the ornaments of a lost civilization in the ruin of a
conquered city, we shuffle the pages of the old stories (about King
Arthur or King George, about Moses and Julius Caesar and the Witch of
Endor) in the hope that maybe, if only we can get them in the right
order, they will yield the gift of meaning. In the meantime, we wait for
Godot or the millennium, equipped with increasingly improved means
toward increasingly incomprehensible ends, bereft of history but surrounded by a collection of marvelous toys, beset by shamans and stock
market touts selling maps of the pilgrim road to the land of virtual
reality.

During the same short week that I tried to read the riddle of Gingrich's book, I ran up against conversations, all of them seriously intended, on the following five topics:

1. Why aliens from outer space (the ones who abduct women from
   suburban shopping malls) have no ears.
2. Last April's bombing of the Alfred P. Murrah Federal Building in
   Oklahoma City revealed as a plot organized by the federal government and meant to revoke the Second Amendment.
3. Whether Oliver North is the reincarnation of the spirit that once
   inhabited the body of Napoleon or the spirit that once inhabited
   the body of Abraham Lincoln.
4. Tomatoes identified as the chief cause for wanton sexual behavior,
   the effects more dramatic in women than in men.
5. The winning numbers in the New York lottery divined by an
   equation taking into account the transits of Venus and the temperature readings, at the Equator, of the Humboldt Current.

Twenty years ago I might have gone to the trouble of making the coun-
terarguments, appealing to the laws of probability or the lessons of
history, but in the faces of my informants (among them a straw-hatted
man in a seersucker suit, two women in flowered dresses, a scholar
possessed of a degree from Harvard) I could read the signs of settled
belief, and I knew that I might as well argue with an elm tree, or with
Gingrich's conviction that before 1965 America was a postcard engraved
by Currier & Ives, or that not until the late twentieth century did it

occur to the nations of the earth to engage in serious and intense economic competition.

To the extent that more people become more frightened of a future that looks a good deal less benign than the one promoted by the Republican Congress, we exchange the force of our own thought for the power of supernatural machines. Doctors of advanced medicine send their patients to the MRI and CAT-scan units in much the same way that Aztec priests brought maiden girls to the deadly altars of Tenochtitlan, and no businessman dares embark upon the voyage of financial speculation without first acquiring a telecommunications capacity so omniscient as to strike terror into the software of his enemies. Let the high school administrator order computer terminals for the sophomore class and, lo and behold, five hundred students, heretofore illiterate, have become educated. Let the money manager mumble the holy words that rhyme with "onics" or "echnics," and lo, the investor has become both rich and wise. In the nation's better shopping malls, the pornographers set up their massage parlors behind neon signs that promise "Compusex" or "Erotics, Ltd.," and on Broadway the successful musicals depend for their applause on brightly burnished dance numbers remarkable for what Arlene Croce once called their "pitiless energy." The interest centers on the complexity of the lights and the speed of the set changes. The same can be said of the popular movies and television serials in which the protagonist turns out to be an automobile, a robot, or a mask. Sensitive to the desperate wish for demigods among the consumers of ready-made myth, the producers of expensive action movies forge the persona of the American hero into an aluminum object impervious to reentry speeds and the heat of the sun.

Hardly anybody knows how to render human character or construct a coherent narrative. The human actors invariably make a mess of things, and were it not for the goodness of a machine (or an old wolf or the Starship *Enterprise),* the poor saps never would win safely through to the IBM commercial. Always it is the technique that counts—the seventy-four modules and twenty-nine functions, the speed of transmission, the seven studio cameras, the placing of the stadium amplifiers, the delicacy of the microphones, the high gloss on the metal. In *To Renew America,* Gingrich achieves the obligatory technological effect by promoting to the status of valves or fuel injectors the "six major changes," the "five basic principles," the "three essential reasons" that operate the engine of social change. When the intended miracle fails to take place—because the systems don't work, or the computer programs prove to be utterly devoid of meaning, or the radar in the B-2 bomber can't tell the difference between a mountain and a cloud—the believers keep their faith intact by pointing to the messy sludge of human emotion that clogs up the workings of the utopian machinery.

Consistent with the slogan "Nobody Beats the Wiz," both the Republican Congress and the Democratic President recommend an electronic device (a.k.a. "the V-chip") as the best means of preserving our dwindling stocks of moral virtue. Their suggestions followed last summer's flurry of worried speeches about the country's continuing loss of innocence. Speaking on the subject in late May in Los Angeles, Senator Robert Dole, the Republican majority leader, blamed the casualties on the news and entertainment media that corrupt the innocent American public with images of sex and violence. "Nightmares of depravity," he said, "... that undermine our character as a nation." President Clinton seconded the motion in Nashville on July 9 ("If we're going to change the American culture, we have to somehow change the media culture") and endorsed a congressional proposal requiring the makers of television sets to install a computer chip capable of blocking out programs tinged with the mark of violence. The technique refers the questions of conscience to particles of magic sand that purify the air, deliver us from evil, and lead us out of temptation and away from the valley of the shadow of death. Carry the research to the next stage of development and with any luck, possibly in time for next year's presidential election, the candidates will be offering corrections for the entire catalogue of human folly and error—microchips that change the *Baywatch* girls into nuns, an L-chip in the library scanning out the intellectual crimes committed by liberal or Marxist authors, R-chips that remove the stains of racism, chips that promote international trade, dissolve the images of adultery into a blur of white static, accept or delete the signals sent by competing astrologers and shopping networks. Morality is a home appliance—like a refrigerator or Gingrich's book—that can be installed in one or more rooms in the house and probably, once the manufacturers learn the rules of the market, in different colors, designs, and wood finishes.

Maybe if we work long enough and hard enough—drawing upon the labor of the newly unemployed and following the architectural designs of the late Albert Speer—we might manage to enclose the whole of the country in a perfect vacuum. So bold a Republican project might strike the fancy of the moralists and hygienists seeking to purify the American body politic, and I can imagine it as a boon to the defense industries depressed by the absence of Star Wars. But even though I'm sure that we could assume the blessing of Pat Robertson and the advice of Alvin Toffler, I'm not sure that we could guarantee the necessary standards of maintenance. Somebody in Cleveland or Texarkana might forget to close a window or shut a door.

September 1995

Eyebrow Pencils

If one wishes to know the real power of the press, one
should pay attention, not to what it says, but to the
way in which it is listened to. ... It only cries so loud
because its audience is becoming deaf.
— ALEXIS DE TOCQUEVILLE

A dvance copies of John F. Kennedy, Jr.'s new political magazine, *George,* appeared on the New York publicity circuit in
early September, addressed by its founding editor to the
kind of people (very upscale, very hip) apt to think—at least until they
meet *George*—that politics are boring and nasty and old. The introduc-
tory press conference took place in Federal Hall, in the rotunda where
George Washington (the magazine's namesake and totem) delivered his
first inaugural address in the spring of 1789. Smiling and at ease in the
company of both the dim past and the shiny present, Kennedy greeted
the assembled gossip columnists and television cameras by saying, "I
don't think that I have seen as many of you in one place since they
announced the results of my first bar exams."

His magazine looked a good deal like *Vanity Fair* or *Vogue* (280 glossy
pages, delicately scented with an assortment of French perfumes), and in
response to questions from the two or three skeptics in the crowd, Kennedy explained (as he also explained in the prefatory note to his 500,000
prospective readers) that *George* was a political magazine from which the
politics had been tactfully removed, "a lifestyle magazine" refreshingly
devoid of ideas and unencumbered by "any partisan perspective—not

even mine," a magazine not unlike a merchandising catalogue "exuber-
antly" and "extravagantly" bent on exhibiting political figures as "pop
icons" and made to the measure of sophisticated consumers certain to
bring to their reading of the Bill of Rights or a speech by Bob Dole the
same standards of judgment (discriminating) and taste (exquisite) that
they bring to their appreciation of an Armani suit, a pair of Ferragamo
shoes, or a Louis Vuitton suitcase.

Consistent with the task at hand, the inaugural issue achieved its
most striking effects with the advertising: 175 pages of stylish photographs representing all the great and glorious names in the retail merchants' Hall of Fame, not only Armani and Ferragamo but also Tommy
Hilfiger, Clinique, Ralph Lauren, Versace, Piaget, Nautica, Valentino,
and Donna Karan—the immortals bringing the gifts of the Magi to a
cradle of democracy.

The editorial drift of the magazine was coordinated with the advertising copy—Cindy Crawford on the cover as George Washington (noble
stance, white powdered wig, eighteenth-century American military uniform, bare midriff, satin ruffle); Cindy Crawford on page 12 (in red silk
on behalf of Revlon's "Fire and Ice"); Cindy Crawford on page 210
telling women in Washington how to dress ("If I were first lady, I'd only
wear black," "Don't get the cheap panty hose," "Tipper's hair is working"). The bulk of the magazine's prose offered a series of variations on
the same tone of voice: up front, under the rubric "Primaries," a few
words about George Washington ("[He] was a big man—big hands, big
feet, big chest"); chatty pieces about the swell parties attended by the
swell new Republican operatives in Washington ("refined strategy ses-
sions for elite leaders" in "genteel" town houses); an account of Julia
Roberts on tour among widows and orphans in Haiti (how Julia suffered
at the hands of the cruel news media and how her good intentions were
rewarded by a waif who said to her, "You're here because you love us");
JFK, Jr. himself interviewing George Wallace, the once-upon-a-time
racist and governor of Alabama (something of a *tour de force* because the
governor is now both deaf and mute); an endpaper entitled "If I Were
President," in which Madonna confesses that "I'd rather eat glass" because as president "one day you wake up and find out that you don't have
a point of view or a set of balls"; a lead essay "The Next American
Revolution Is Now") in which the novelist Caleb Carr promotes the new
American political season in language suitable to a report from Paris on
the autumn clothes, informing the friends of *George* that when they

really stop to think about "all the great issues and events of our day," they, too, will discover what he and John F. Kennedy, Jr. and Isaac Mizrahi and Newt Gingrich's lesbian half-sister and Liz Claiborne and Gianfranco Ferre already know: that politics are where it's at.

But if politics were where it's at, who would have time for *George*—a political magazine without the politics and with a fashion model for its muse of fire? Why write letters to the editor with an eyebrow pencil? The questions kept coming to mind as I made my way through the text, and by the time I reached the last four-color photograph (of Madonna swallowing a goldfish) I understood that the magazine would have been more appropriately dedicated to the sacred memory of George III. Here was an expensive collection of celebrities fetchingly arranged in the homespun poses of democratic self-government, but who were the people whom *George* was meant to astonish or impress, and where was the audience for a magazine presenting as its chief virtue the great news that it had nothing to say?

Politics are by definition partisan, because they constitute an argument about power—about who gets to do what to whom, under what circumstances, and for how long and with what degrees of objection or consent. Castrate the quarrel, divorce politics from any meaning that cannot be sold in Bloomingdale's, and what is left except a round of applause for William Kristol's tie and Cindy Crawford's hair?

Kennedy, in his prefatory note, speaks of a "freshly engaged public" and a boisterous crowd of presumptive readers "energized by their anger" and eager to indulge "their passion for politics." He might as well have been referring to the immense crowd of well-adjusted and perfectly conditioned people on Planet Reebok. During the 1994 election—the one that all the swell people in the first issue of *George* were talking about as the Second Coming of Christ the Republican—no more than 39 percent of the electorate turned up at the polls, and of those who did, only 25 percent knew the names of their senators or representatives. The country's genuinely political journals circulate among small numbers of readers, and few television public affairs programs command audiences large enough to qualify for a single ratings point. I don't know what kind of crowds the editors of *George* encounter on the great American plains, but in my own wanderings around the country over the last several years I've noticed that without the backing of the Christian Coalition or the addition of large celebrity (personages on the order of

Elizabeth Taylor or Henry Kissinger) political meetings tend to consist of twenty or thirty people whose hair isn't working, seated on folding chairs in a small room, asking questions either bitterly partisan, hopelessly irrelevant, or terminally paranoid—studio audiences sometimes positioned for the C-SPAN cameras to suggest the illusion of a quorum.

The general lack of interest in political affairs corresponds to the general disaffection for anything and everything modified by the adjective "public." For twenty years the drum majors of the Republican parade band have been beating time to the same ideological refrain—private schools, private prisons, private suburbs, private roads, private money, private police—and by now even the crippled remnant of the Democratic Party has come to acknowledge the sovereignty of private means over public ends. All things bright and beautiful flow forth from the clear mountain streams of the private sector; all things vicious and ugly rise from the swamp of the public sector. Power derives its legitimacy and authority from the mints of private wealth, not from the coinage of public thought, and people who once might have thought of themselves as citizens now tend to think of themselves as the vassals of a commercial overlord.

Corporations of the magnitude of IBM or Citibank constitute themselves as what Renaissance Europe would have recognized as city-states, sovereign powers employing as many people as once lived in Philadelphia in 1789. When it suits their interests, they send their agents to Congress (as they did last spring with respect to the telecommunications and environmental bills) to write the necessary laws. A man without a company name is a man without a country; it is no longer the political commonwealth that furnishes him with a pension, medical insurance, club membership, credit cards, meaning, and a common store of experience. As recently as a hundred years ago most Americans lived in small towns arranged around a public square or green, a community consisting of a school, a courthouse, and a church, and our range of observation was available free of charge. Now we must pay for what goes by the name of common experience at the stadium, the cineplex, or the mall, and we define ourselves as the sum of our possessions or the collection of our ticket stubs.

George proceeds from the assumption that the important political decisions take place in private (at the Federal Reserve Board, on one of the Disney Company's airplanes, over breakfast at the Willard Hotel), that what Versace has to say (even in Italian) is a good deal more inter-

esting than who gets elected president of the United States or what the
Congress says to itself about the balanced budget or the war in Bosnia.
But in the meantime somebody has to keep up appearances, maintain
the fiction of a national political debate, make lists of Senator Alfonse
D'Amato's favorite songs and pasta dishes, organize the props and lights
for what John F. Kennedy, Jr. (again in his prefatory note and attributing
his insight to his lifelong access to the best seats in the American grand-
stand) calls "the giant puppet show that can turn public people into
barely recognizable symbols of themselves."

On or about the same day that Kennedy introduced his new magazine to
the ladies and gentlemen of the press in Federal Hall, General Colin
Powell set forth on a twenty-five-city tour to promote his autobiogra-
phy, *My American Journey,* and the two events were as well matched as
Cindy Crawford's accessories—a political campaign that wasn't a political campaign, a post-partisan candidate refreshingly devoid of controver-
sial views, a politician from whom the politics had been tactfully removed, a fall fashion statement (noble stance, twentieth-century
military uniform, firm jaw, many medals) made to fit the cover of everybody's magazine. The news media hustled the general into the limelight
with the effusive haste of a starving mob in a besieged city welcoming
the arrival of a relief column. The country was said to be in desperate
straits, exhibiting ominous signs of moral rot and social decay, and here
at hand was a great captain embodying all the old-time American virtues believed to have gone AWOL from a Saigon bar in the summer of
1969. Within a matter of a few days in September, Powell appeared
before the talk-show cameras with Barbara Walters and Jay Leno, *Time*
magazine published a 7,500-word excerpt from the Random House
book (500,000 copies shipped, $6 million author's advance), and news-
paper columnists of all persuasions abandoned themselves to a frenzy of
praise—"classic soldier-statesman," "a president for all seasons," "tran-
scends politics," "photographic memory." Powell not only was a hero—a
man who had "power-walked" with Presidents Reagan, Bush, and Clinton—but he was also black, "America's black Eisenhower." Not *too*
black, of course, not so black that he would scare anybody, but black
enough to stand as a symbol of payment for a long-overdue debt, allowing white people to imagine—at least for the time being and while
being questioned by the opinion polls—that they were tolerant and kind
and wise, so emancipated from racial prejudice that they could seriously

entertain the prospect of a black man in the White House.

In the small print behind the dress uniform and the glittering adjectives, the general didn't quite come up to the promise of the ad copy. A deft and self-promoting careerist, he apparently had risen through the ranks by never doing or saying anything that ruffled the surface of the consensus already present in the briefing room, an officer so disinclined to take risks that he worked out a doctrine of guaranteed victory, committing the United States Army only to those wars that it could easily win (preferably in deserts, never in mountains), a military bureaucrat so skilled in the arts of camouflage that in Vietnam in 1968 he adroitly delayed discovery of the My Lai massacre, and in Washington in 1986, on the staff of the secretary of defense, he arranged the illegal transfer of arms to Iran, blandly failing to recall (114 times) any knowledge of the event at the subsequent congressional hearings—in brief and in sum, an accommodating man who once told the *Washington Post* that "issues come and go" but "process" lives forever.

Nor did his book, or at least those fragments of it that I read in *Time,* contradict the impression of a latter-day Polonius. The general told the story of his life as a series of uplifting homilies consistent with the plot lines of television situation comedy—strong family ties, up from poverty in the South Bronx by dint of good conduct and hard work, off to the army, which he embraced as "my home … my life … my love," aide-de-camp to a series of important people in and around the White House, lots of power-walking, chairman of the Joint Chiefs of Staff. On the questions that threatened to veer off into the swamp of politics, the general let issues come and go and stayed steadfastly with process. Yes, he had "Republican leanings," but he was also "a New Deal kid"—conservative but not too conservative, a believer in "discipline" but also a strong supporter of "compassion," vague about abortion and capital gains taxes, solidly in favor of mother and the flag.

Reading the general's text, I remembered having once been told that during the fall of 1941, when German tanks had advanced to within ten miles of Moscow, the managers of the Soviet Union placed a wax dummy of Joseph Stalin in a lighted window of the Kremlin, high enough up off the street to escape close inspection but near enough to sustain the illusion of a godlike presence. Stalin the man might have been in a bomb shelter or the Crimea, but Stalin the wax figure, tireless in his labors and impervious to fear, remained stolidly at his post, the great leader alone in his study, seated calmly at his desk, directing the armies in the field, and summoning from the impregnable soil of Mother Russia the strength of 10,000 armored divisions.

The United States in the autumn of 1995 isn't as badly off as Moscow in October 1941, but still it is a comfort to see Colin Powell and Cindy Crawford high up in the lighted windows of the news media and to know that if they really put their minds to it, either singly or together, they could probably summon from the pages of the imperishable American past the mighty spirit ("big hands, big feet, big chest") of *George*.

November 1995

Christmas Carol

You can tell the ideals of a nation by its advertisements.
—NORMAN DOUGLAS

Wandering among the remote shelves of a Fifth Avenue bookstore in late October, I came across a small stack of books on the floor near a freight elevator, ten or twelve copies of a cheaply printed paperback bound up with string and marked with a slip of paper identifying them as goods in transit. Assuming that they were what was left of the summer's best-selling news about the O. J. Simpson trial, and curious to see which authors and what theories of criminal justice were being returned to pulp, I lifted the corner of the invoice and was surprised to find Charles Dickens's *A Christmas Carol* in a red cover with the familiar illustration of Mr. Fezziwig's ball. I had mistaken the direction of the shipment. Books that I had thought were going out were coming in, but the sales clerks apparently hadn't decided where to place what the publisher's tag line described as "the most beloved Christmas tale of them all."

As I continued to browse among the season's newest political tracts, many of them about bringing discipline to the nation's economy and strengthening its penal codes, it occurred to me that maybe the clerks were embarrassed by the mawkish sentimentality of the beloved tale. Maybe they were reluctant to display it in the front of a store that undoubtedly numbered among its patrons quite a few corporate managers apt to possess precisely those qualities that Dickens so deplored in Ebenezer Scrooge—"Hard and sharp as flint, from which no steel had ever struck out generous fire, secret, and self-contained, and solitary as an oyster." It won't do these days to make a mockery of wealth or portray a rich businessman as anything other than a hero of the people. Money is the proof of grace, and a miser, as every schoolchild knows, is a great and good conservative. The plot line of A Christmas Carol didn't fit the bracing spirit of the times, and neither did its irresponsible moral lesson. Here was old Scrooge, an exemplary Republican, troubled in his sleep by ghostly dreams of human kindness, changed into a gibbering liberal at the sight of a crippled child. Hardly an inspiring tale of triumphant profit-taking and certainly not one that anybody would want to place next to a handsome photograph of Newt Gingrich or Peter Lynch.

Sensitive to the predicament of the sales staff, I wondered whether it might be possible to rewrite A Christmas Carol in a way that more nearly matched the forthright, manly teaching of the Contract with America. Not an easy revision, of course, and one that would require some fairly heavy-handed deconstruction of the text, but after a few moments' thought, and taking heart from the brisk sales at the cash register of Beyond Prozac and Your Sacred Self, I understood that the tale was probably best retold as a sequel. As follows:

STAVE I

Our story begins with the appalling sight of Ebenezer T. Scrooge V, a benign and mild-mannered man in his late fifties, generous to a fault, who for many years has been squandering his great-great-grandfather's noble fortune on misguided schemes to rescue the unrepentant poor. The imbecile philanthropist sits reading a romantic novel by Leo Tolstoy in a small but cheerful library surrounded by the worthless tokens of an idealist's misspent life—photographs signed by Mahatma Gandhi, Gary Hart, and Hillary Clinton, civic awards mounted in second-rate silver, a pet owl, forgotten reports from forgotten presidential commissions appointed to study racial injustice and environmental disgrace, Mark Twain's walking stick, books published by Marxist university professors, framed letters of appreciation from the students of an elementary school in Ciudad Juárez, a bowl of Hudson River mud.

It is the hour after sunset on Christmas Eve, and the rest of the house is full of music and light. The children and grandchildren of Ebenezer Scrooge V, all of them too careless with money (too careless by far) and too easily moved to laughter (to the point of impertinence), have invited so many guests to dinner that they can't remember how many places to set at the table. They make a joyful noise of their preparations, the clattering of plates and the popping of champagne corks joined with the sound of a piano and three voices singing "God Rest Ye Merry Gentlemen."

The ghost of Jacob Marley drifts through the library door looking as dismal as it looked in London in 1843, "like a bad lobster in a dark cellar," but instead of being weighted down with heavy locks and chains, the apparition takes the form of a scolding family lawyer come to correct the spendthrift heir with the switch of sound advice. Scrooge suggests a glass of wine, "a little something to restore the color to your cheeks," but Marley waves the offer impatiently aside and reminds the descendant of his former partner that the money is all but gone, the trust funds nearly exhausted, and the warehouses on the verge of bankruptcy. Before floating out the window, the ghost tells Scrooge to expect three unearthly visitors, three spirits who, if he heeds them well, will recall him to the bosom of Mammon.

STAVE II

The Ghost of Christmas Past bears a remarkable resemblance to John D. Rockefeller, the founder of the fortune of that name and known during his long and grasping life as the incarnation of stinginess. Somber as a pallbearer, looking more like a starved New England clergyman than a well-fed financier, the ghost bids Scrooge rise from his chair and walk with him in the night sky on a grand tour of America as it existed a hundred years ago, the old, economically competitive America, innocent of labor unions and free of feminists. The spirit shows Scrooge a series of canonical scenes: gangs of Chinese laborers laying railroad track across the Nevada desert, handsome policemen mounted on thoroughbred horses suppressing Irish mobs, criminals on treadmills, unheated shoe factories in the dead of winter, the children bent to their tasks in orderly and uncomplaining rows, patriotic newspapermen wearing checked suits and bowler hats, bowing like kewpie dolls to the magnates of the Gilded Age, grim country parsons singing psalms, picturesque beggars in sprightly rags, indigent pensioners dying as unobtrusively as flies, too proud of their American heritage (independent and self-reliant) to bother anybody with a plea for help or a cry of pain.

Presented as an album of prints by Currier & Ives, the little scenes blink on and off at regular intervals through the scudding cloud, and to each of them the Ghost of Christmas Past affixes, like a Christmas ribbon or a sprig of holly, the ornament of an edifying thought:

"Beware, Ebenezer Scrooge, the ageless ingratitude of the poor."

"Never show sympathy to people from whom you can expect nothing in return."

"Charity destroys initiative and rots the will to industry and enterprise."

Scrooge stands abashed before the solemn images of frugality and thrift. For the first time in his wastrel's life, he begins to apprehend the majesty of a cold and savage heart, and when the spirit returns him to the comfort of his library he glances at the fire burning on the hearth and thinks that it would cast a purer light with one log instead of four.

STAVE III

No sooner has the clock struck the hour of ten than the Ghost of Christmas Present rises up through the floor like the genie from Aladdin's Lamp—a figure not dissimilar to that of Rush Limbaugh or Roseanne—grinning, corpulent, and huge, the soul of perfect selfishness. Dressed in a loose gown of flowered silk and wearing on its gigantic head a crown of cloves and pineapples, the apparition claps Scrooge boisterously on the back and announces, amid gusts of booming laughter, that it has come to teach the lessons of gratified desire. Only fools and saints and New Deal Democrats subordinate their own comforts to those of others or put off until tomorrow pleasures that can be seized today. So saying, and as if to prove its point, the great spirit seizes Scrooge by the wrist, drags him upward through the roof, and spreads before him a second panoramic view of America the Beautiful. Once again the purpose is didactic, but instead of dwelling on the triumphs of the past, the genie of the shopper's lamp displays the glories of the miraculous present. The settings are all suburban—office parks and shopping malls, resort communities protected by high walls and iron gates, ski lodges, university quadrangles, boat marinas. No black or brown people appear anywhere in sight—no red or yellow people, nobody wearing rings in his ear or her nose, no loud musical instruments, no government bureaucrats, no street vendors selling filthy foreign foods. All the factories have been turned into overpriced restaurants, all the assembly lines neatly trimmed and downsized (like the hedges at the entrance of a good hotel), all the IRS agents turned into tennis instructors or personal trainers.

Enfolding Scrooge within the giant arc of its ham-like arm, and with a chuckle as merry as the holiday catalogue from Bloomingdale's, the Ghost of Christmas Present invites him to gaze upon the prizes that money buys for people mature enough to know that in the end and when all is said and done (no matter what happens to anybody in Bosnia or Queens), they have only themselves to please. From the depths of the now starry night a magnificent procession of shining luxuries floats before Scrooge's eyes, and as the objects pass splendidly by, the great spirit names them as the orphaned pleasures that Scrooge has foolishly forsworn.

The last yacht and the last cashmere cap drift slowly away to the south, and Scrooge once again discovers himself in his library listlessly turning the pages of a book that suddenly seems as dingy and old as Leo Tolstoy's beard. It occurs to him that maybe he has lived too long in the company of the dispossessed. As a child he had known about the marble fountains and the heavy motor cars, and he had seen magazine advertisements for the racehorses and Italian suits, but the second unearthly visitor had surprised him with some of the newer and more complicated toys—menageries of tame politicians in silver cages, miniature billionaires no bigger than fawns, newspaper editors cleverly contrived to sing like the golden, mechanical birds once made for the amusement of Oriental princes.

STAVE IV

In the hour before midnight the Spirit of Christmas Yet to Come, an ominous and silent figure in a black shroud, summons Scrooge with the gesture of one outstretched hand—a hand as pale as death—to the French doors leading out into the rose garden. Scrooge has by now become wary of strange sights. Guessing at the nature of the dreadful entertainment likely to appear among the rosebushes, he rises unwillingly from his chair, afraid to look upon the face of doom. In a small and creeping voice he asks for program notes: "You are about to show me shadows of things that have not happened but will happen in the time before us? Is that so, Spirit?"

The phantom neither speaks nor moves. The outstretched hand draws back the curtain of the night, and the garden blooms with scenes of pandemonium that look like they might have been jointly painted by Jan Brueghel and Hieronymus Bosch: the entire population of Oklahoma stoned on drugs and heavy metal rock bands loose in the Iowa corn, undocumented aliens disembarking from ships (like the animals descending from Noah's ark) in every port on the once well-defended American coast, unemployed corporate executives (white and middle-aged) selling apples on the steps of the Pentagon, lewd women (as young and licentious as Calvin Klein's child models, as old and insatiable as the Wife of Bath) selling sexual favors in Harvard Yard, gay and lesbian parades in Salt Lake City, debates in Congress conducted in gangsta rap, fifth-grade classrooms studying the history of pornographic film (a twenty-seven-part series produced by the Public Broadcasting System and narrated by Bill Moyers), shiftless fathers throwing away their children like empty beer cans, unwed mothers nursing unbaptised infants on the floor of the New York Stock Exchange, altar boys spinning roulette wheels and nobody reading William Bennett's *Book of Virtues,* young black men in velvet top hats standing around on street corners frightening the police.

Scrooge cannot bear to look upon the dreadful scene for more than twenty minutes. He falls trembling to his knees, clutching at the phantom's robe. "Hear me, good Spirit. Why show me this if I am past all hope? I am not the man I was. I will not be the man I must have been but for this gift of Phil Gramm's grace."

The phantom departs as silently as it came, and the exhausted Scrooge falls into a fitful sleep, dreaming of reform schools.

STAVE V

Faithful to the miracle of redemption, Scrooge awakens on Christmas morning restored to the winter glory of his ancestors—his cheeks noticeably shrivelled, his blood four degrees colder in his stiffened veins, a suddenly squeezing, wrenching, envious man whose movements have become as quick and nervous as a lizard's tongue. At last Scrooge has come to know the meaning of a dollar and the beauty of the bottom line. In a hurry to be up and dressed, his hands busy with his shirt and tie while at the same time talking on a cellular phone, he cancels the clown ordered for a children's cancer ward, instructs his brokers to buy shares in companies that own and manage prisons, orders the closing of seven factories, chases out of the house the company of useless guests, berates the cook (for putting too much stuffing in the Christmas turkey), disinherits his grandchildren, and sells the owl. Later in the morning, on the way to his office in New York City, Scrooge walks briskly north on Fifth Avenue, shaking his shrunken fists at the Christmas wreaths but coveting, like any other loyal American, all the precious merchandise in all the better stores. Asked for money at the corner of Fifty-seventh Street by a crippled child as surely doomed as Tiny Tim Cratchit, Scrooge rebukes the waif for its insolence and kicks away its crutch.

December 1995

Time Lines

Life must be lived forwards, but can only
be understood backwards.

— KIERKEGAARD

Assume that the existence of the American democracy requires the existence of an electorate that knows something
about American history, and last November's press release
from the U.S. Department of Education can be read as a coroner's report.
The government's examiners questioned 22,000 schoolchildren in fifty
states about their knowledge of the nation's past, and after arranging the
answers as a set of charts, they returned a finding of mortal ignorance:
more than 50 percent of all high school seniors unaware of the Cold War,
nearly six in ten bereft of even a primitive understanding of where
America came from, only one in every hundred capable of placing General Custer's last stand on the hill in Montana on the same geopolitical
horizon with Colonel Roosevelt's assault, twenty-two years later, on the
hill in Cuba. Although the report card showed a better grasp of history
among grammar school students than among high school students, it
revealed few important differences between students of different gen-
ders, races, or economic strata.

It wasn't as if anybody had expected the news to be good. For the last
twenty years the ministers of the nation's educational affairs (university
deans as well as federal bureaucrats) have been reporting signs of decay—low SAT scores, dwindling verbal aptitudes, a general inability to
find Tokyo on a map—and like the falling grades in all the other sub-

jects, the poor marks in history didn't mean that Old Glory wouldn't continue to float in the orange-scented breeze over the Rose Bowl. It's a nice flag and a rich country, and nobody expected the stock market to collapse because a lot of high school seniors didn't know the difference between a Federalist and a Pequot Indian. American schoolchildren never have been fond of textbooks, choosing whenever possible to follow Huckleberry Finn south and out of town, and their inattention didn't foretell the sudden disappearance of Revlon, Microsoft, and the professional golf tour.

What the report card did mean was that the schools have lost the thread of the American narrative, and that without that narrative the country cannot long sustain the appearance, much less the substance, of democratic self-government—not because everybody needs to remember the *Maine* or the Alamo but because as Americans we have no other way of knowing ourselves. Unlike every other nation in the world, the United States defines itself as a hypothesis and constitutes itself as an argument. Other nations make do with shared bloodlines, a common store of language, inherited portfolios of ancestral myth reaching backward in time to the first Irishman or the first Korean. But as Americans we have only the dialectic in which we try to frame the opposing principles of liberty and equality into a political architecture that best supports the cause of freedom. The founders of the American republic devoted themselves to the study of history because they knew that they had nothing else on which to build the future except the blueprint of the past. Well aware of both the continuity and contingency of human affairs, Adams and Madison searched the works of Tacitus and Voltaire and Locke like carpenters rummaging through their assortment of tools, knowing that all the pediments were jury-rigged, all the inscriptions provisional, all the alliances temporary.

If we no longer hold the study of history in such passionate regard, it's because we like to think of our political institutions as monuments or museum pieces, completed works in a past tense, and if American schoolchildren believe that Squanto is a rock group, it's because they live in a society that thinks of history as ornament and stage design—a subject fit for interior decorators and best rendered as a theme park.

The government report card aroused a fair number of the country's newspaper columnists to cries of indignant alarm—America falling behind in the economic competition with Germany and Japan, the schools failing to deliver high-quality product to the infrastructure, etc.—but my own feeling was nearer to sorrow. I sent for the government's report, and behind the bleak walls of institutional prose, I could all too easily imagine cell blocks K through 12 in which history appears as a collection of old stones or a cabinet of dead birds. The government examiners had asked their questions in the stunted language of multiple choice (For five points, which of the following was one of the original thirteen colonies?), and it was clear that even if the children had got the answers right, they had been poorly served, disarmed as citizens and denied their inheritance as the beneficiaries of the whole of the human story.

When taught by a teacher who knows what he or she is about, the imaginative taking up of the experience of the past can be put through as many paces as a well-trained circus horse. The study of history furnishes what Dionysius of Halicarnassus praised as "philosophy learned by example," instills a sense of humor, wards off what Hamlet decried as "the slings and arrows of outrageous fortune," allows the citizens of a democracy to know the difference between their enemies and their friends.

People unfamiliar with the world in time find themselves marooned in the ceaselessly dissolving and therefore terrifying present, divorced from both the future and the past, surrounded by the siege of images in the mirrors of the news. The mass media promote the impression that the urgent questions of the moment (war in Bosnia, corruption in Washington, crime in Los Angeles) arrive like monstrous apparitions, uninvited and unannounced, from the Land of Mordor. The spectators forget how and why events come to pass, and not knowing where to find their place in the human story (in Chapter 12 or on page 438), condemned to a state of constant dread, they become an audience fit for the market in three-day wonders and one-line jokes.

I narrowly escaped recruitment into the same claque. Although I was lucky enough to attend private schools, the higher fees by no means guaranteed a higher order of instruction, and among all the history teachers from whom I took notes over the span of sixteen years, I remember only two who brought to their subject the gifts of passion and talent. In my mind's eye I see them both as clearly as the paper on which I'm writing this sentence. Mr. Mulholland stands at the blackboard in a seventh-grade classroom in San Francisco, a heavy and florid man given to broad gestures and sudden shouts, drawing the line of Hannibal's elephants through the valleys of Cisalpine Gaul. The chalk squeaks, and the annals of ancient Rome come as vividly to life as the sound of the ball game in progress under the windows on Jackson Street. Mr. Mulholland spends a week on the Carthaginian descent into Italy, another week at the bend in the river near Cannae, a month on the Punic Wars, six months on the destruction of the Roman republic and the contrived divinity of Caesar Augustus. Never once does his voice tire or his enthusiasm fail. He tells the story as if it happened yesterday in Golden Gate Park, stringing together a coherent narrative from different phyla of meaning, different kingdoms of fact: a military expedition in Scythia reminds him of something Pliny said about jackals at a dinner party in Pompeii; discussing the logistics of the Egyptian grain trade, he remembers how bitterly Juvenal resented Egyptian barbers; and before the hour ends he has improvised a philippic against Cleopatra and the Ptolemies. On Monday he compares and contrasts the deaths of Cicero and Seneca; on Tuesday he describes Trimalchio's banquet and Ovid's exile on the Black Sea; on Wednesday he draws the moral about how hard it was to tell the truth in Imperial Rome and still dine on plover's eggs.

Mr. Garside, whom I encountered in my third year at boarding school in northwestern Connecticut, paces back and forth in front of the arched windows that overlook the golf course, his voice high and thin and vaguely British, his clothes eccentric, and his manner foppish—a man easily mocked for what at first seemed like the affectations of an actor appearing in a play by Oscar Wilde. His genius for telling stories dispels the suspicion of the class, and by the end of the fall term the muffled witticisms in the back row have given way to awe. Much younger than Mr. Mulholland, Mr. Garside has been engaged to teach modern European literature, but he is also studying for a doctorate at a university from which he has taken temporary leave, and he cannot suppress the impulse to extend his observations about Dickens or Flaubert to further remarks about Victorian England and the comic-opera empire of Napoleon III. I can still see him, forty years ago on a warm October afternoon, pausing slightly before he makes his customary turn under the window with a broken pane, about to describe Dickens's morbid wandering through the Paris morgue during the same week in June 1863 that the Army of Northern Virginia was moving north toward Gettysburg and the Duke de Morny (the principal conspirator in the coup d'état of 1851 and a mountebank of whom Mr. Garside was particularly fond) was gambling away his wife's fortune at the roulette tables in Biarritz.

At Yale University I entertained but soon abandoned the thought of becoming a historian. Even as long ago as the 1950s the study of history was sinking into the mire of heavily footnoted research, the life and times of Lincoln or Alexander the Great beginning to disappear into a fog of abstract nouns that sounded like translations from a German treatise on postindustrial socioeconomic theory. History is only intelligible as narrative (which is why the Department of Education noticed a better grasp of the subject among very small children), but narrative these days is against the university rules. People who tell stories cannot avoid making judgments—about character, motive, the nature of right and wrong. Judgments imply opinions, which bring up questions of politics, which embarrass the deans and the Development Office.

Given the bias against the telling of stories, I'm astonished that anybody learns anything at all, but I still cannot help thinking of people without a sense of history as orphans. Deprived of the feeling of kinship with a larger whole and a wider self, and unable to fix their position on the map of time, they don't know that the story in the old books is also their own. How, then, do they make sense of what they read in the newspapers, much less heed the counsel of the dead, or marshal the strength of their own minds against what G. K. Chesterton called "the small and arrogant oligarchy of those who merely happen to be walking around"?

Were it not for the gauge of history, I wouldn't know how to measure the emptiness of what now passes for political statement on the television news. On the same day that I read the Department of Education's report card, I came across several orators from the Rocky Mountain states boasting to the CNN cameras of the regional traits of character (self-reliance, rugged individualism, etc.) that allow the cattle to safely roam, and if I hadn't known something about the settling of the trans-Mississippi West I would have missed the joke. The westward course of American empire was conceived and organized as a public-works project, entirely dependent (then as now) on the government dole. By 1845 everybody traveling west on the Oregon or Santa Fe Trails understood that the new country was rich in five primary resources—land, minerals, furs, timber, and government subsidy—and that of these, the last was by far the easiest to reach and exploit. The federal treasury supplied funds for every improvement that anybody could name (railroads, dams, forts, river channels, mining and fishing rights, irrigation canals, orange groves), and the trick (now as then) was to know the right people in Washington or the county courthouse. The West was won less by the force of independent mind than by the lying government contract, the crooked lawsuit, the worthless Indian treaty. The entire chronicle of the western adventure rings with the whining voices of the not-so-sturdy pioneers, blaming their misfortunes on somebody else, never on their own stupidity and greed. The sound was as unpleasant then as it is now, and somehow by knowing that it is not new, I can more easily bear the effrontery of Phil Gramm.

Similarly, when I read in the papers that the mass media have corrupted the American mind with the shows of violence, I remember that in the 1840s prosperous farmers in small midwestern towns (i.e., the *fons* and *origo* of Dan Quayle's family values) brought picnics and small children to public hangings. At conferences sponsored by the World Policy Institute or the Council on Foreign Relations, I listen to important newspaper columnists urge the sending of American troops to Bosnia because the Serbian bullies must be punished to discourage other bullies elsewhere in the world, and I think not only of the same important columnists making the same fatuous remarks prior to the American expedition in Vietnam but also of the slaveholding southern gentry in Charleston in April 1861, drinking triumphal toasts on the night before the Confederate artillery fired on Fort Sumter. In Central Park I see Pope John Paul II blessing the crowds gathered in the sheep meadow, and instead of thinking his message as pious and sweet as the sentiment on a Hallmark card, I remember how the flock of the faithful was winnowed by the good shepherds of the Spanish Inquisition.

Because we live in an age demanding of miracles and grand simplifications, I would have thought that the study of history deserved a fairly high place in anybody's curriculum. I'm told that the number of people in the United States at the moment who believe in the literal truth of the biblical Book of Revelation exceeds the number of people who lived in all of medieval Christendom, and in a newspaper the other day I noticed that a voodoo priestess in New Orleans by the name of Sallie Ann Glassman was seeking to rid the city of crack cocaine through the good offices of Ogoun La Flambeau, a god of war and fire, whom she had summoned from the forests with an offering of rum, gunpowder, and old graveyard dirt. At Harvard University a professor of psychiatry verifies the sighting of intergalactic aliens, and other seers at other microphones speak of Zionist cabals, of balanced budgets and zero debt, of the Trilateral Commission deploying black helicopters to harass the settlements of virtue in eastern Idaho. Across all the world's twenty-four time zones the adherents of one or another of the ancient superstitions wage their furious assaults on what for the last two hundred years has been known as the spirit of the Enlightenment. Against the vivid cries and promises of transcendence, we have little else with which to preserve and extend the work of civilization except the voices of experience. Defined as means rather than end, history defends the future against the past.

January 1996

Sacred Scroll

What we wanted, we did not know;
what we knew, we did not want.
—ERNST VON SALOMON

O ver the course of a presidential election year I expect the books published on political themes to read like the speeches at a Fourth of July picnic—heartwarming cant as plentiful as the beer and as empty as the balloons—but six weeks before the New Hampshire primaries I discovered *The Frozen Republic: How the Constitution Is Paralyzing Democracy,* by Daniel Lazare, to be the exception that proves the rule. In the sanctuary of the American civil religion nothing except a private fortune in excess of $5 billion is more precious than the four pages of parchment brought forth by the corporate sponsors of liberty in Philadelphia in the summer of 1787. Lazare, an accomplished iconoclast, manages within the space of a few hundred pages to assign them to the realm of magical objects in which a museum of natural history also might place the totem poles, the scraps of sacred moleskin, and the bones of a departed saint. I'm not enough of a constitutional scholar to find the flaws in Lazare's legal reasoning, but his knowledge of American history is as persuasive as his wit, and despite his lack of academic connections and his provenience in the often ideological left (as a columnist for *The Village Voice* and the New York editor of *In These Times),* I was glad to encounter a writer willing to suggest that only by reconfiguring our system of government (i.e., by rewriting the Constitution) can we address what by now have become the all too obvious consequences of our political weakness and stupidity.

The proposition seems to me to stand as proven in any morning's newspaper. At least one story in every four speaks to the presence of a constitutional crisis that we pretend not to notice but which accurately defines the enfeebled state of our national politics—the federal government twice shut down in the early winter because of a quarrel about a balanced budget (i.e., a metaphysical dispute about a set of wholly imaginary numbers), the futility of a Congress unable to negotiate a disarmament treaty with a citizenry possessed of 200 million guns, the selling off of the public lands despite the objections of at least 60 percent of the nominally sovereign American people, the notion of legitimate political authority so far from anybody's mind that the office of the presidency can be bought at a price well below that of a second-rate record company or a losing football team.

Lazare arranges his polemic in historical sequence—the origins of the Constitution as a marvel of eighteenth-century political mechanics made to the design of seventeenth-century religious belief, the impious (and unanswerable) questions forced on its infallible authority by the Civil War, the desperate denials of the document's obvious imperfections during the era of American ascendance following the victories in the Second World War, the blind worship of the sacred text that has accompanied the last fifty years of the country's descent into bankruptcy and the wisdom of Rush Limbaugh. Three of Lazare's points about the obsolete and undemocratic character of the Constitution strike me as useful glosses on a presidential election year likely to present the owner of *Forbes* magazine as the friend of the common man.

Virtuous Incapacity

Listening to a politician talk, or while reading an indignant editorial in an earnest newspaper, the trusting citizen might make the mistake of thinking that the government was supposed to work—as if political power were a form of energy (like diesel fuel or department store credit) meant to be used for a constructive purpose. The supposition is false, but it gives rise to the chorus of complaint (about crime and drugs and federal fraud, or the cities falling into ruins and the suburbs foundering in the morass of debt, or the failures of will and the lack of ennobling moral vision) that accompanies the ritual of an American election. The complaints goad the candidates to promises of reform, which supply the news media with headlines, but have nothing to do with anything other than their own reflection in the public opinion polls.

The government was never supposed to work, at least not in the ways imagined by a municipal planning commission. The political shambles is deliberate, and the government's incompetence a testimony to its virtue. The gentlemen who wrote the Constitution were as suspicious of efficient government as they were wary of democracy, a "turbulence and a folly" that they associated with the unruly ignorance of an urban mob. They looked upon political power as a corrupting substance—in much the same way that William Bennett and Pat Buchanan look upon the evil of crack cocaine-and they belonged by temperament to what in seventeenth-century England would have been understood as the "Country Party"—well-to-do gentry, many of them Puritans, who opposed, on principle as well as for reasons of interest, what was known as the "Court Party." Lazare cites Lawrence Stone's *The Causes of the English Revolution* on the division between the two parties, a division that continues to define, much to our misfortune and nearly 350 years after Charles I lost his head, the ideal and anti-ideal of the American political dream:

> [The Country] was peaceful and clean, a place of grass and trees and birds, the city was ugly and dirty and noisy, a place of clattering carts and coaches, coal dust and smog, and piles of human excrement. ... the Country was virtuous, the Court wicked; the Country was thrifty, the Court extravagant; the Country was honest, the Court corrupt; the Country was chaste and heterosexual, the Court promiscuous and homosexual; the Country was sober, the Court drunken ... the Country was outspoken, the Court sycophantic; the Country was the defender of the old ways and old liberties, the Court the promoter of administrative novelties and new tyrannical practices. ...

Like their descendants on both our own Arcadian left and Suburban right, the wealthy American planters and merchants who wrote the Constitution associated themselves with the purity of the Country Party. Believing themselves morally and intellectually superior to the democratic rabble, they defined the practice of government as the duty of the judicious few to control and improve the instincts of the foolish many, and they undertook to render the federal political power as impotent as a eunuch in the court of a Ming emperor. Power was to be kept out of the hands of children (a.k.a. the sovereign people) and away from anybody as likely as Alexander Hamilton to make of government an efficient instru-

ment of intelligible purpose. Hamilton was a forward-looking man who
assumed that the events looming below the horizon of the future would
best be met by a strong government and a flexible constitution. Jefferson
imagined that America in 1900 would look much the way it looked in
1800, and with more or less the same pastoral prospect in mind the
editorial committee in Philadelphia conceived the portrait of the American future as a romantic reconstruction of the Roman or Tudor past.
Toward that idyllic end they produced a government weak enough to
preserve the institution of slavery and a Constitution rigid enough to
resist the invasions of social change. The Preamble granted unlimited
powers to "We the People," but Article V (the clause that makes amendment virtually impossible by requiring a two-thirds vote in both houses
of Congress and ratification by three fourths of the states) declared the
Preamble null and void. Denied the means of revising what suddenly
had become an immutable and ancient law, the newly independent
Americans enjoyed even less freedom to alter the course of their destiny
than the subjects of George III.

Balanced Impotence

By containing the powers of government in a mechanism as finely balanced as a late-seventeenth-century ornamental clock, the authors of the
Constitution distributed political energy among so many weights and
counterweights that nobody could say for certain how the movement
originated or where sovereignty was to be found. Let the several functions of government work at cross purposes (the legislature against the
executive, the executive against the legislature, and the judiciary against
anyone it chose), and with any luck they would hold one another indefinitely at bay. Political power divided into as many parts as the fragments
of the True Cross couldn't interfere with the economic power, and the
marvelous state of suspended animation served everybody's interest as
long as everybody agreed that the private good was another name for the
public good. But the practice of keeping slaves presented the gentlemen
in Philadelphia with a contradiction for which their Constitution had no
answer (human liberty on the one hand, private property on the other),
and the absence of a political means of addressing the question resulted,
seventy-four years later, in the Civil War and more than 600,000 dead.

Contrary to Lord Acton's often quoted dictum about the corruption inherent in absolute power (that is, the "tyrannous and arbitrary power" dreaded by the eighteenth-century American gentry and reviled by the teachers of twentieth-century American civics lessons), concentrated power can be plainly seen and (if the opposition has the courage to do so) held to account. Power broken into a thousand pieces can be hidden and disowned. If no individual or institution possesses the authority to act without the consent of everybody else in the room, then nobody is ever at fault if anything goes wrong. Congress can blame the President, the President can blame the Congress or the Supreme Court, the Supreme Court can blame the Mexicans or the weather in Ohio. Checked and balanced by powers of all denominations, the country's public servants become, in theory, accountable to everybody; in practice they remain accountable to nobody, "dithering and indecisive, borne aloft on great billows of empty rhetoric," free to strike attractive moral attitudes while at the same time selling their votes to the highest corporate bidder. By further complicating the proceedings with congressional committees and subcommittees (now numbering nearly 300) and a myriad of federal, state, regulatory, regional, and district government entities blessed with the authority to levy and collect taxes (at last count numbering at least 83,000 in the United States), the machinery of divided government disperses even the semblance of responsibility into a haze of impotent recrimination.

The God in the Machine

Lazare traces the fervor of our present constitutional devotions to the complacence that settled on the American mind in the years immediately following the Second World War, and he begins his chapter on the consequences of that complacence with the observation that "the only thing more dangerous than total defeat is total victory." The winning of the war prompted the Americans to think that their military and industrial supremacy was proof of their moral and political virtue, and by 1953 Daniel Boorstin, the historian soon to become the Librarian of Congress, was attributing what he called "the genius of American politics" to Divine Providence: "[I]t is not surprising that we have no enthusiasm for plans to make society over. We have actually made a new society without a plan. Or, more precisely, why should we make a five-year plan for ourselves when God seems to have had a thousand-year plan ready for us?"

Almost everybody else in the country at the time, Democrat and
Republican as well as liberal and conservative, held to similar be-
liefs—God was in his heaven, all was right in the world, America was
great because it was America, and the Constitution had been brought to
Washington in a glass box by the Archangel Gabriel. The less fortunate
nations of the earth might have to suffer the indignity of realigning their
political thought with the events of the second half of the twentieth
century—in the last fifty years new constitutions have appeared in Germany, France, Portugal, Holland, Sweden, Denmark, Russia, and Japan—but the Americans, being American and therefore perfect, could
afford to look upon the stately passing of recorded time with the serene
indifference of Mt. Rushmore. What was the point of thinking seriously
about politics when the country was being governed, as it had always
been governed, by the magic parchment in the museum with George
Washington's inkwell and Benjamin Franklin's wig?

The United States in the meantime fell behind every other country in
the industrialized world in most of the categories that measure the
well-being of a civilized society: the most brutal police force and the
most crowded prisons, the harshest system of criminal justice, repressive
drug laws, a lazy and sycophantic press. Over the span of the same fifty
years our political campaigns have come to resemble nothing so much as
games of trivial pursuit, charades reduced to works of performance art in
which the candidates smear one another with insults instead of chocolate.

All observations about the country falling off its marble pedestal were
met by referrals to the Constitution. America was still the wonder of the
world because our wealth made us wise, and because in its handsome
display case in Washington, as miraculous as the engines aboard the
Starship *Enterprise,* the Constitution was protecting, by day as by night,
the liberties of its chosen people. The assumption renders any further
effort at political thought both unnecessary and impious.

Theocratic societies tend to have a weak grasp of reality, and toward
the end of his book, remarking on the fulminations of the Country Party
presently holding the majority in Congress, Lazare says: "All those Republican House freshmen in early 1995 who could be seen sporting
copies of the Federalist Papers were not all that different from Iranian
mullahs waving copies of the Koran."

A historian rather than a political scientist or a first-year congressman, Lazare doesn't offer a set of instructions for redrafting the Constitution, but he carries his point about our idolatrous worship of the document, depriving us of the courage to imagine a future that doesn't look like one of the Disney Company's replicas of the nonexistent American past. The framers of the Constitution lived in a world innocent of electricity, jet aircraft, telephones, computers, nuclear weapons, and MTV; if their political mechanism had already become outworn by the middle of the nineteenth century (that is, incapable of resolving the question of slavery), then how can we expect it to address the questions likely to be presented by the twenty-first century?

Maybe we would be better served by a government more nearly resembling Britain's parliamentary system, and I suspect that we would be well advised to take from the Supreme Court the privilege of judicial review and rework the undemocratic electoral equation whereby each state elects two senators no matter how small its population. But we can't engage in the conversation unless we rid ourselves of our documentary superstitions, and until we begin to talk about revising the structure of American government, our political debate amounts to little more than a twittering of opinion polls about which candidate has the most money, the fewest felony convictions, and the best hairdresser.

March 1996

Capitalist Tool

In democracies, nothing is greater or more brilliant
than commerce. It attracts the attention of the public and
fills the imagination of the multitude.
— Alexis de Tocqueville

When I listen to Steve Forbes make political speeches, I think of my Great-aunt Evelyn, who, at the age of sixty-three, took up a career as an opera singer. Nobody in the family ever understood why she did so, but she was a woman of substantial wealth and impervious to suggestions (very hesitant and modest suggestions) that she possessed no talent for her chosen art. Her whims descended upon her in sudden gusts of inspiration, and one summer afternoon, without prior warning or explanation, she installed on her estate in Connecticut a maestro imported from the basement at La Scala. For the next eighteen months, wandering through the halls of the house in which the servants fled the sound of her approach, she practiced her scales and trills and sang, in a wavering mezzo-soprano voice, the arias of Giacomo Puccini and Christoph Willibald Gluck. When the maestro pronounced her the equal of Renata Tebaldi, she hired Town Hall for her New York debut. The performance wasn't as well attended as Forbes's progress through the New Hampshire snow, but what the audience lacked in size and camera equipment, it made up for with the fervor of buoyant expectations that filled the first five rows of an otherwise empty auditorium. Aunt Evelyn was no fool, and she had taken the precaution of informing her friends, relatives, and dependents that anybody marked absent for the evening would be omitted from her will.

The concert lasted nearly three hours, without what the Italian maestro regarded as the indulgence of an intermission. Holding herself firmly erect in front of the grand piano, wearing a black dress and a necklace suggestive of ancient Egyptian royalty, Aunt Evelyn brought forth her entire repertoire (arranged in historical order from operas of Monteverdi to those of Richard Wagner), and never once did she sing five consecutive notes in the same key. Every now and then she made an inexplicably abrupt and imperious gesture with the palm frond that served as her only prop.

Forbes displayed a similar awkwardness in front of the C-SPAN cameras, but his determination was as unblinking as Aunt Evelyn's, and so was his serene indifference to the prospect of ridicule. Although obviously unfamiliar with public places and uneasy in crowds, he was a man so seized by the glory of the flat tax that he bravely endured what he called "the hazing of the American political system" and stoically ignored the reports of his campaign having foundered on the shoals of the Iowa caucuses. Watching him exhibit his collection of reactionary economic theory (not only the flat tax but also the return to the gold standard, the long-lost Laffer curve, and the maxims of Friedrich von Hayek), I thought of an amiably myopic British peer earnestly showing the weekend guests his prize poultry, and I couldn't see in him the character of vile usurper preferred by his rival candidates and a quorum of the country's important newspaper columnists. The invective of Senator Bob Dole I could ascribe to the envy of a politician unendowed with limitless supplies of money, but the press criticism had about it an air of churlish ingratitude.

Here was an affable and well-intentioned citizen, furiously riding his hobbyhorse around a course of New England shopping malls, providing, at his own not inconsiderable expense, a civic entertainment meant to teach a lesson in the noble art of American self-government. So many and so generous were the gifts of his campaign that none of the attending journalists lacked occasion for a witticism or a sermon. The humorists compared him to a glass owl, a bobbing-head doll in the back of a car, a giant white rabbit, a toy robot, and an enameled Easter egg; the moralists pointed to his presumption as proof that money had so besmudged the polished brightwork of the American political machinery that the presidency had become an office as easily bought as a municipal judgeship or a seat in the United States Senate. Nobody had the grace to say that the candidate and his money might have wandered off into less public-spirited directions, that while Forbes was pursuing his political pastime in New Hampshire, John Eleuthère du Pont (the heir to another magnificent American fortune) lost one of the Olympic wrestlers whom he had been tending like a flock of merino sheep, on his estate in suburban Pennsylvania.

Wealth in sufficient measure grants its possessors the right to their enthusiasms, and if they can afford to rent a concert hall or hire Johnnie Cochran in, on what ground is it possible to quarrel with the dreams of self projected in the mirrors of the news? More often than not the equestrian classes occupy themselves with animals and architecture (Aaron Spelling's house in Westwood, the late Doris Duke's pet camels, etc.), but a certain kind of rich man prefers the pleasures of moral or political dandyism. He feels obliged to hold views, espouse causes, restore order. The spectacle is nearly always comic—H. Ross Perot as a latter-day Oliver Cromwell, Michael Huffington come to rescue California from the sin of pride, Donald Trump at the zenith of his celebrity in the middle 1980s buying full-page advertisements in the *New York Times* to explain his thinking about Japan; Mortimer Zuckerman acquiring *U.S. News & World Report* for $185 million (a sum nearly double that of the going rate for the presidency) in order to appoint himself resident sage as well as editor in chief. Most newly arrived publishers at least have the wit to regard their property as a kind of very expensive rubber duck, and they content themselves with giving lunches for wandering dignitaries and deciding the broad questions of national policy. Zuckerman had it in mind to make a grander entrance into the intellectual limelight. Week after week, traveling to Moscow before the Geneva Summit Conference or to Manila just after the revolution, he returned with breathless discoveries of the obvious—"Readiness for war is part of the problem as well as part of the solution," or, more urgently, "Pre-emptive surrender is not good negotiating doctrine."

What was remarkable about the Forbes campaign was neither the candidate's vanity not his tendency to speak of himself in the third person, bout the willing suspensions of disbelief granted both to his impersonation of a populist and his promise of a new economic dawn. Striking the two poses simultaneously—the sudden lurching of his left hand uncannily reminiscent of Aunt Evelyn's palm frond, Forbes stood before his fairground audiences in Manchester or Concord as a friend of the common man, threatening to "drive a stake through [the] heart" of the tax code, railing against the corrupt "lackeys" and "politicians" in Washington who were forever milking the elk of honest American labor.

It was an earnest speech and undoubtedly heartfelt, but it belonged, like Aunt Evelyn's opera singing, to the surrealist school of public declamation. The system that Forbes denounced was the one to which he owed his fortune and his boyish grin—the system under which he pays an annual property tax of $2,111 on a 520-acre farm in Bedminster, New Jersey, and sets the price of a weekend's political jaunt at a sum equivalent to what most everybody else in his democratic audience could expect to earn in a year. Forbes improved upon the surrealistic effect by proposing as a remedy for the country's economic distress precisely those measures that under the direction of the Reagan Administration had run the annual deficit from $79 billion in 1981 to $290 billion in 1992 —i.e., a bankrupt economic theory dressed up with a new set of feathers (eliminating all deductions and taxes on interest, pensions, dividends, inheritance and capital gains) certain to vastly enhance the wealth and power of a grasping plutocracy from which the candidate in the expensive blue suit promised to retrieve the ladies and gentlemen wearing quilted parkas and bomber jackets.

But no tumultous questions drifted forward to the podium and no angry voice rose up in the back row of the gym. The silence was respectful, the shaking of the candidate's hand as reverend as the kissing of a cardinal's ring. I thought of Aunt Evelyn coming mercifully to the end of her first concert, the audience rising to its feet in a storm of tumultuous applause, and the cries of "Brava" echoing through the empty hall. The accompanist bowed deeply before the wonder of the diva's art. A destitute nephew presented a bouquet of roses for which he had pawned his watch. A threadbare niece was heard to remark that never before had she understood the importance of Gluck.

Admiring Forbes's repeated escapes from the mockery of his imagined peers, it occurred to me that he owed his standing in the polls not simply to the sum of money that he had paid for his campaign (some $14 million in the last three months of 1995, $6 million in the first six weeks of 1996), nor even to the sunny optimism of his pre-recorded message about the "spiritual renewal" and "economic boom" awaiting his fellow countrymen over the horizon of the next election, but to his personification of the American dream. When a man as rich as Forbes stands revealed in the full glory of a net worth of $439 million, it is as if Mammon himself had stepped off the bus from Portsmouth, America is a nation of expectant capitalists, all of us hoping to join the company of the monied immortals who can play at being gods and do anything they wish—drive fast cars, charter four-masted sailing vessels, produce movies, drink the wine of orgy and campaign for political office—and here at last was a man who had drawn the winning number in the lottery of birth.

Word of Forbes's fortune preceded him like a brass band or a pillar of fire. The media were careful to confine their jokes and moralisms to the editorial page; the front-page stories preferred to inventory the candidate's store of earthly treasure—a palace in Tangier, the estate in New Jersey decorated with the picturesque comings and goings of the Essex Fox Hounds and the Tewksbury Foot Bassetts, houses in New York and London, an art collection, a chateau in France, a mountain in Colorado, an island in Tahiti. Best and most wonderful of all, Forbes himself was so untroubled by the worries of ordinary men that when asked by the *Wall Street Journal* to reflect on the trials and obstacles of his life, he was hard put to remember any. Working backwards in time past the memory of inheriting his father's magazine and his incarnation as a Princeton student, he came at last to his leaving home for a New England prep school, a challenging adventure that had taught him, he said, "why pioneers went out."

Because Forbes's fortune had come to him from the divine cloud that also had descended upon the Mellons and the du Ponts, it wouldn't have mattered if he had been made of tin or carved in wood. Like Presidents Kennedy and Reagan, the candidate had about him an air of reassuring opulence, a little stiff perhaps and overly pleased with his own escapade, but familiar with the comforts of the safer suburbs and knowing that it is the lot of the successful American politician to put a smiling face on the imperatives of property.

As I watched Forbes blandly turn aside the questions asked of him by Ted Koppel and Larry King, I remembered not only Aunt Evelyn's concert but the Senate Rules Committee in the autumn of 1974 questioning the Nelson Rockefeller about his fitness for the vice presidency of the United States. Rockefeller had been appointed to that office by President Gerald Ford, and in full view of a nation still alarmed by Richard Nixon's betrayal of the public trust, not a single senator could bring himself to ask a hard question. Overcome with awe in the presence of Rockefeller's fortune, even the skeptics on the committee prostrated themselves before the witness like slaves staring into Pharaoh's golden face.

The complex mechanisms of the modern world depend as certainly on the faith in money as the structures of the medieval world depended on the faith in God. To the extent that the society employs an intrinsically worthless medium of exchange—paper or numbers on a screen instead of gold or land or furs—the expansion of its wealth demands increasingly daring suspensions of disbelief. The flesh becomes word, and the numbers come together in poetic metaphors. Make the numbers big enough, and then make them immanent in all the world's credit cards, and people will believe almost anything—even Steve Forbes dressed up as a populist or the promise of a happy return to the good old days in America when nobody, not even Andrew Carnegie, was forced to swallow the insult of an income tax.

The newspaper columnists who worried about what was to become of Thomas Jefferson's republic and Andrew Jackson's democracy in an age of virtual reality wrote testy editorials about the American presidency being sold at auction to any rich sportsman with a taste for summit conferences instead of polo ponies. Their fretting seemed to me as vain as their complaints about Forbes's lack of a public record. No man ever comes to the White House with sufficient wisdom or experience, and unless we change the campaign finance laws—allowing individual citizens to contribute a good deal more than $1,000 to candidates whom they admire—who else except the very rich can afford the costs of the television promotions while at the same time keeping up the appearance of moral virtue and independent mind?

The entrance onto the national political stage of so many wealthy amateurs suggests that the holding of public office has become largely ceremonial—a matter of knowing which fork to select at a state dinner, when to smile and how to read a script, where to stand for the photo op, and how to present to the American people an image of dignity and calm. Given our American belief that money is the alpha and omega of human existence and the god from which all blessings flow, who better to serve as Pontifex Maximus and chief priest of the American civil religion than a figure already encased in gold?

As herald of the opulent new morning in America, Forbes is probably too early in the field to win the prize of the White House. Like Aunt

Evelyn, who abandoned her concert career after three seasons and five voice teachers, he presumably will discover other means of expressing his concern for his fellow man. Aunt Evelyn devoted the latter part of her life to the growing of geraniums, and maybe Forbes will take up the collecting of butterflies or stamps.

April 1996

Balzac's Garret

Heard melodies are sweet, but those unheard
Are sweeter; therefore, ye soft pipes, play on.
— JOHN KEATS, "Ode on a Grecian Urn"

As a poor and unpublished writer in Paris in the early 1820s, Honoré de Balzac lived in a meager garret under a roof of broken tiles near the cemetery of Père Lachaise. The landlord provided nothing other than a table, a bed, and a chair, and so Balzac, who was fond of luxury, dressed the room in words. On a stained and empty wall he inscribed the notice "Rosewood paneling with commode"; on the opposite wall, equally bare, "Gobelin tapestry with Venetian mirror"; and in the place of honor over the cold fireplace, "Picture by Raphael." Twenty years later, having become both famous and rich, Balzac filled his several apartments and townhouses with the literal-minded proofs of his once impoverished hypothesis—mirrors both Venetian and French, Sèvres porcelain, picture by Delacroix.

The progression from fantastic wish to literal fact followed the plot of what until recently would have been recognized as a standard American success—young man of promise storms the walls of the capital city, climbs the ladder of ambition, gives weight and form to the images of his desire, makes his way across the dance floor of the best society, and achieves the stature of a commodity. The story is no longer so standard, and if I can believe what I read in the papers about the numbers of people whose economic well-being has been eliminated or much reduced, the line of the narrative has turned back on itself—middle-aged pillar of the community falls through the trapdoor of an unforeseen merger, descends the stair of humiliation, withdraws to a garden apartment near a suburban freeway, and there contents himself with the heartening or poetic notices posted on the Internet.

The friends of the new global economic order haven't yet gotten around to promoting the changed direction of the American journey—away from the fertile plain of well-watered department stores and into the desert of metaphysics—but they make a solemn show of worrying about what's to become of the once-prosperous American middle class, and in another two or three years I expect that we will begin to see the travel posters: COME TO THE LAND OF MAKE-BELIEVE. TAKE HEART IN THE THINGS OF THE SPIRIT. REJOICE IN WHAT ISN'T THERE.

The good news should prove easy to sell. The longing for the ineffable and the unseen has been characteristic of the American mind since the beginning—as present in the seventeenth-century Puritan settlements on Massachusetts Bay as among the pilgrims moving west across the trans-Mississippi frontier in the 1840s or departing for Paris in the 1920s to join the legion of the lost generation—and it is a mistake to think of the Americans as a materialist people. Foreign or leftist observers like to imagine the United States as a caricature of a nineteenth-century plutocrat, an obese gentleman in a waistcoat and top hat devouring the fruits of honest labor as if they were truffles in the mouth of a pig. The emphasis on earthly appetite misses the point, and the critics who deplore the rapacious American consumption of superfluous goods fail to notice that more often than not the material acquisitions serve as tickets of admission to the desired states of immateriality. The taste of the truffle matters less than what the eating of the truffle represents—i.e., induction into the company of the elect and a place at the table of self-esteem.

We are a people captivated by the power and romance of metaphor, forever seeking the invisible through the imagery of the visible. Even if we assemble what the world is pleased to acknowledge as a fortune, we discover that it fails to satisfy the hunger of our spiritual expectation. As Tocqueville long ago noticed, "The Americans clutch everything but hold nothing fast, and lose grip as they hurry after some new delight," which explains why we never get quite all the way to the end of the American dream and accounts for the feeling of vague melancholy that echoes like a blues rhythm through the back rooms of so many American success stories.

Other than to people seeking to prove or grasp what isn't there, to whom does Pat Buchanan present his nostalgic tent-show pageant of America the Beautiful or Senator Alfonse D'Amato the congressional excitements of the Whitewater investigation? As of early March, the Senate search for swindlers and dance-hall girls on the upper reaches of the Whitewater River had run a course of 300 days (the longest hearings ever held by the U.S. Congress and a good deal more extensive than either the Watergate or Iran-Contra hearings), produced 45,000 documents and 132 witnesses, and still had failed to discover a single proof of wrongdoing on the part of either President or Hillary Clinton. Attempting to replicate the heroics of Teddy Roosevelt, Buchanan manages the bravado of General George A. Custer, but his pose is no more or less absurd than that of Colin Powell (a supple careerist and bureaucratic courtier) as a statesman of independent mind, or that of H. Ross Perot (who made his fortune as a government contractor) as a populist come against the corruptions of Washington. The painted melodrama is traditional, but without an audience of born metaphysicians the Hollywood movie studios wouldn't have become the eighth wonder of an admiring world and no American political campaign could move its circus wagon to the next town or the next opinion poll.

The land of make-believe has been well mapped by four generations of advertising copywriters, and as they have improved their knowledge of the terrain, so have they learned that it is the naming rather than the making of a thing that draws a crowd. They sell the symbols of happiness or immortality at the counters of abstraction, and the slogan, the designer label, the celebrity endorsement, and the corporate trademark come to embody not only the immortal soul of a product but also almost the entire sum of its commercial worth. Just as the unheard melodies of Keats's Grecian urn fill out the implied harmonies of American politics, so also they stock the better stores and shopping malls with celebrated brand names disguised as skirts or shoes or shaving cream. At the higher elevations of abstraction, both word and image need refer to nothing other than themselves. Ringo Starr, formerly drummer to the Beatles, received $1 million from a Japanese advertising agency last winter merely to state his name in a beer commercial, and when Michael Jordan announced his return to the Chicago Bulls in 1995, share prices of the five corporations for which he serves as pitchman (among them McDonald's, Nike, and Gatorade) gained a combined value of $1 billion on the New York Stock Exchange. Sometimes, of course, symbolism fails, and what the Lord giveth, the Lord taketh away. Random House agreed to pay Joan Collins $4 million to write a novel that it reclassified as worthless drivel when she delivered the manuscript three years later—not because the visible text was anything other than expected but because its invisible subtext had blown away with the soap bubble of her fame.

As commodities increasingly come to consist of little else except information, even the sensual pleasures of the flesh drift off into the spheres of abstraction. Adulterous love affairs take place in cyberspace, and the brothels reconfigure their displays of sexual temptation as a suite of voices talking on a telephone. The going rates at the better resort hotels have less to do with the view of the mountains or the sea than with the soft pipes of flattery playing in the golf shop or the spa; the managers of expensive restaurants give more thought to the composing of the menu than to the cooking of the trout. The Chicago Board of Trade sells options on next summer's hurricanes, and baseball teams sign contracts for $10 and $20 million with stumbling outfielders unlikely to hit better than .250 in the hope that so expensive an advertisement for an imaginary prowess will bring fans to the ballpark and quickness to the player's bat. Books on spiritual or inspirational themes, often told in the voices of angels, sell far more copies than books written by even the most renowned secular humanist. Within the last two or three years the authors of pulp fiction have discovered what is known as "the Christian thriller," and Pat Robertson, founder of the Christian Coalition and once-upon-a-time candidate for president, published a novel in the form last summer under the title *The End of the Age,* in which his hero describes the events preliminary to the second coming of Christ, among them a meteor falling on Los Angeles and the Antichrist at large in the White House. The novel sold 275,000 copies.

Like the evangelist and the retail merchant, the politician and the bond-market tout seek to endow information with the character of a tangible commodity, and their art, which is a literary one, consists in persuading the faithful to see visions not unlike those vouchsafed to the early Christian saints. Year after year the country's most eminent economists make predictions consistently ridiculed by events; year after year the brokerage firms sell hundreds of millions of shares in companies that go nowhere but south; year after year the editors of investment newsletters charge handsome fees for advice that is as worthless as the geopolitical theory published in the policy journals. Nobody minds because it is understood that the learned gentlemen speak and write an unintelligible language not unlike church Latin, and in the meantime the Dow Jones average continues to rise because the customers hear the unheard dance music on the painted surface of a stockbroker's reassuring smile.

Given both the transcendental bias of the American mind and the genius of modern communications technology, I expect that in the not too distant future we can look forward, in Max Frisch's phrase, to "arranging the world so that we don't have to experience it." If it is true, as Marshall McLuhan suspected, that "travel now differs very little from going to a movie or turning the pages of a magazine," then we never come to any new place, and to the extent that we live within the little rooms of the electronic media (i.e., in Balzac's garret) everything becomes a name posted on a wall, a Web site, or a television screen. The habit of abstraction would explain not only Ralph Lauren's fortune and Pat Buchanan's presidential campaign but also the state of disrepair into which the United States has let fall its highways, its schools, its railroads, its cities and public squares. If the media are nothing more than the means of storing and transporting information, and if by assuming the character of information, commodities can be moved by fiber optics, fax machines, and ATM cards, then why bother to maintain an infrastructure made to the specifications of medieval Europe or ancient Rome?

Or why go to the trouble of preserving the logistics of a consumer society that depends on the moving of so many cumbersome goods that the once-prosperous American middle classes no longer can afford to buy? It is both easier and cheaper to deliver the image of a thing instead of the thing itself, and the substitution of the lighter for the heavier object conforms to the fashionable trend of the times—in line not only with the downsizing of corpulent business corporations but also with the passions for fat-free diets, the ascetic doctrines of the Eastern religions, portable offices, clothes designed to express the look of stylish poverty, and the aesthetics of minimalist art. Let enough people learn to regard the acts of reduced consumption as attenuated, postmodern forms of the full-blooded pagan ritual of getting and spending once practiced by their forefathers in the Christmas-tree forests of the 1950s, and maybe they will come to know that even the smallest bottle of perfume from Versace or Dior contains within it the dread and ancient spirit of Mammon, in much the same way that the dry crust of the Communion wafer embodies the flesh of Christ.

As Americans we make of the sermon, the sales pitch, and the lawsuit our principal forms of literary expression, and I don't doubt that the next generation of the avant-garde will prove itself capable of redefining the notion of property. Microsoft already owns electronic rights to works by Rembrandt and Da Vinci as well as those by Raphael and Delacroix, and in the newspaper a few years ago I noticed that a lawyer arguing a case about a shipwreck off the coast of South Carolina had hit upon the principles of "tele-possession" and "tele-presence." If I understand the theory correctly, it might be possible to carry the feasts of consumption into the realm of the surreal. The SS *Central America,* on a voyage from San Francisco to New York in 1857, sank in a hurricane with a cargo of gold, and the submersible robot sent by a syndicate of latter-day prospectors to search the wreck at a depth of 8,000 feet returned with photographs offered by the syndicates as proof of title. To the best of my knowledge the case is still making its way through the courts, but if the principle of tele-possession is eventually upheld, who then owns Elizabeth Taylor or the Empire State Building?

To citizens of eighteenth-century Paris too poor to buy bread, Marie Antoinette offered the famous suggestion of eating cake. Her counterparts in the palaces of late-twentieth-century capitalism—relying on what I'm told are the wonders of interactive media—might suggest the eating of pictures of cake. Even now, at almost any hour of the day or night, the cable television networks offer a buffet of food and cooking programs, many of them watched in lieu of chocolate by women on a diet, and the manufacturers of jogging shoes sell 70 percent of their product to people who don't jog.

The larger task of redirecting the American journey back from the kingdom of literal fact to the provinces of fantastic wish I expect to proceed along more or less the same lines as a presidential election campaign. Although the candidates travel around the country presenting themselves for photographs in the midst of cheering crowds, in effect they stand in an empty television studio under a ceiling of acoustic tiles. The corporate overlord provides a table, a camera, and a chair, and the authors hired for the occasion dress the room in words. On one of the blank walls they inscribe the notice, "Speedboat with gold fittings"; on the opposite wall, "California vineyard with movie star"; and, in the place of honor, behind the candidate's head, "Pictures by Walt Disney."

May 1996

Citizen Dole

New ideas are for the most part like bad sixpences,
and we spend our lives trying to pass them off on one another.
—SAMUEL BUTLER

*O*n the evening of May 15 the television networks broadcast
and rebroadcast Bob Dole's tearful farewell to the U.S. Senate in so many variations (as sound bite, extended fragment,
complete performance) that well before midnight I knew that I was in
the presence of what the literary critics describe as an iconic text. An old
and threadbare politician was dressing himself up in a new suit of images, attempting the miracle of metamorphosis and setting up the story
lines for the summer presidential campaign, and if it so happened that
the miracle came to pass and brought about his election next November,
all the authorities would agree that it was this speech, this sudden and
dramatic change of costume, that set him on the road to victory.

It was an artful speech artfully delivered, as cynical as it was false,
expressive of the senator's contempt (for himself as well as for the people
to whom he was speaking), but after seeing it for the third time I didn't
know whether I was angry or sad. Here was a man telling yet another lie
to people whose best hopes he repeatedly had betrayed, but his yearning
for the presidency was so desperate and so nakedly exposed that I was
prompted to a feeling in the vicinity of pity. The senator's thirty-five
years in Congress had schooled him to the bit of humiliation—how to
cadge for votes and beg the scraps of corporate campaign money, how to
buy and sell this year's principles and last year's friends—and he stood

93

before the cameras as obligingly as a photographer's model, willing to
wear whatever face he was told to wear, happy to try on a fetching smile
or another hat. Apparently he had something pious in mind—maybe
something along the lines of a medieval knight swearing the vow of
chastity and taking the cross of Holy Crusade, or St. Francis of Assisi
wandering away on a mule to comfort a quorum of lepers, but in any
event a grandly humble gesture meant to signify his deliverance from
the iniquity of Washington and his going off into a Kansas sunset to find
the lost wells of American innocence.

By and large the news media took the senator at his word (it being in
their interest to promote the entertainment value of the election campaign), and the next day in the *New York Times* William Safire approved
the resignation from the Senate ("gutsy," "adept"), applauded the speech
("terrific," "eloquent"), and expressed the hope (dear to the hearts of all
loyal Republicans) that a morally re-awakened candidate might put to
rout the despised President Clinton. Variations of the same sentiment
decorated the op-ed pages of the country's conservative press as well as
the Republican aisles of Congress. Albert R. Hunt of the *Wall Street
Journal* thought the speech "picture perfect," and Arianna Huffington,
speaking on behalf of Orange County and the *New York Post,* was reminded of the Norse god Wotan, sacrificing his left eye in return for
inner wisdom. Speaker of the House Newt Gingrich praised Dole's courage ("frankly, a bolder move than I could have counseled"), and Senator
Alan Simpson of Wyoming told reporters gathered in the Senate Rotunda that soon they would behold marvels in the western sky: "He's
unshackled. All the leg irons are off. We've snatched the hood from a
falcon."

Although I don't like to think so, it is conceivable that the American
people are as stupid as Senator Dole believes, and maybe they will prove
themselves deserving of his scorn by sending him to the White House.
Even so, the cynicism of his goodbye seems to me worth the trouble of
an explication. From the top:

"Let me say ..."
The senator presents the voice of the speech as his own, as if the words
had come to him in a dark night of the soul when his campaign managers inadvertently left him alone with the rustlings of his conscience. He
maintains the fiction of the first-person singular throughout the text ("I

will seek …," "I will then stand …," "I will begin …"), but the voice was bought and paid for in the upscale markets for ornamental prose that also supply the Washington carriage trade with earnest moralism and impromptu after-dinner jokes—the speech written by a contributor to the *Wall Street Journal,* the delivery rehearsed for many days in front of a mirror under the direction of a drama coach, the message approved by the Republican National Committee, the tone of personal anguish tested in the wind tunnel that measures the probable force and direction of the opinion polls.

"I will seek the Presidency with nothing to fall back on but the judgment of the people and nowhere to go but the White House or home."
The sentence divides into two propositions, both disingenuous and one of them revolting. Unlike the vast majority of his fellow citizens, whose wages have failed to keep pace with inflation over the last twenty years (people who have lost their professions as well as their jobs and mortgages), the senator can fall back on the appreciation of the corporate patrons whom he served during his terms in Congress in the capacity of loyal and faithful gamekeeper. Comfortably established in Washington and Bal Harbour, Florida (the second address acquired on favorable terms from the Archer Daniels Midland Corporation, which has received upward of $40 billion in federal subsidies since 1979), Dole can look forward to a succession of handsome rewards—generous lecture fees, club memberships, invitations to become a partner in a prominent law firm or sit among the directors of companies capable of furnishing the privileges to which he was accustomed as majority leader.

The second clause elaborates the mockery. The senator begs the sympathy and admiration of the American people (all too many of whom lack decent food, shelter, or medical care) for bravely facing up to the harrowing choice between the luxuries of the White House and the comforts of a Florida resort. What a stalwart fellow ("gutsy," "terrific," "picture perfect"); how courageously he turns up the frayed collar of his orphan's coat and strides nobly forth into the storm of a cruel and unforgiving world.

"So my campaign for the Presidency is not merely about obtaining office."
The campaign is about nothing else except obtaining office. During the spring primary elections Dole was so eager for votes that he sold at discount prices his entire stock of moral and intellectual scruple. He

color-coordinated his view on abortion with the bigotry of the Christian Coalition; embraced, repudiated, and again embraced the cause of gay rights; set aside his enthusiasm for a balanced budget; borrowed from Steve Forbes the theory of a flat tax and from Pat Buchanan the howling (suitably muted) about American capital stealing the bread of American labor. So shameless was Dole's snatching at any straw in the wind that Buchanan took to entertaining his audiences with a mechanical parrot (a.k.a. "the Bobster") programmed to repeat whatever he said on the topic of the day. When moved to high-pitched moral statement, the parrot flapped its toy wings. But the Bobster was a captive of Washington politics, and now that it has been unshackled, its leg irons struck off, and the hood snatched from its head, it is free to repeat anybody's message.

"It's about fundamental things, consequential things, things that are real."
Made of three evasive adjectives and an abstract noun, the phrase could as easily refer to a Chevrolet truck or a case of Miller beer. It allows the candidate to keep all his options open in the hope that he or one of his new speechwriters will think of something to say that might be construed (if only for a sound bite's duration on the Wichita evening news) as fundamental, consequential, or real. The task is by no means easy. During the seven months of campaigning before quitting Congress, the two most notable issues with which the senator associated himself (the return of the Cold War and the repeal of the gas tax) were both rooted in fantasy, and his two most memorable attempts at visionary statement were sufficiently vacant to serve any purpose and all occasions—"We can do better" and "Our future is ahead of us."

"My campaign is about telling the truth."
No political campaign (not now, not fifty or one hundred years ago) is about telling the truth.

"It's about doing what is right."
The campaign, like all campaigns, is about doing what's expedient. If it runs true to Republican form, it will consist of little else except the smearing of President Clinton with the mud of rumor and innuendo—Clinton's sexual misadventures, Clinton's missing war record, Clinton as grinning liar and pillar of sand, Clinton's encouragement of abortionists, Clinton's appointment of a surgeon general who mentioned

masturbation, Clinton's shrewish wife.

Against the background of the Democratic Sodom on the Potomac, the newly redeemed Dole will strike the poses of high moral character, the man of courage and integrity whose campaign pays top market price for the season's crop of raw and distilled slander.

"It's about electing a President who's not attracted to the glories of office but rather to its difficulties."
If Dole had been attracted to the difficulties of public life, he would have remained in Washington. The office of Senate majority leader, in many ways more glorious than that of president, provides a broad range of legislative powers as well as a podium from which to define the purpose of government. Dole's conception of the office was that of a head waiter. Having no notion of the future that wasn't a re-run of the past, and not knowing what it was that he wanted to say or do (other than to preserve the status quo and keep all the paper moving in the proper direction), he made a shambles of the Republican political agenda. On two occasions last winter his dithering over partisan points of doctrine brought the federal government to a standstill. Embarrassed by Gingrich, outmaneuvered by Clinton, made ridiculous by the news media, Dole abandoned the difficulties of office as if they were a sinking ship or the scene of a crime.

"To leave behind all the trappings of power, all comfort and all security."
Other than the pope or a sovereign head of state, no man travels with more security, in more comfort, and with heavier trappings of power than an American presidential candidate nominated by one of the two dominant parties. The would-be tribune of the people moves between photo opportunities with the pomp and ceremony of a seventeenth-century monarch, preceded by motorcycles, surrounded by sirens and Secret Service agents, accompanied by a train of aides-de-camp, attended by a sycophantic press. And to what end? Not to renounce, as Dole's speechwriter implies, the corruption of Washington and the sin of pride, but to return to Washington as promptly as possible and there to enjoy more trappings, more comfort and security, more power.

"And I will then stand before you without office or authority, a private citizen, a Kansan, an American, just a man."
Alas, poor Dole, who was once a god. Like Jesus of Nazareth, he consents

to wear the rags of mortality (for at least six months) in order to rescue the people of Zion from eternal damnation. But the tone of voice is self-pitying instead of magnanimous, and the senator as everyman sounds like Shakespeare's Richard II—a pathetic and deluded king, making dust his paper and writing sorrow on the bosom of the earth, saying to his courtiers, "I live with bread like you, feel want, taste grief, need friends. Subjected thus, how can you say to me I am a king?" William Safire can say so, and so can Arianna Huffington.

"I will seek the bright light and open spaces of this beautiful country and will ask for the wise counsel of its people, from the seacoasts of Maine and California to the old railroad towns in the Midwest. ..."
A sarcasm. The disdain implicit in the senator's speech presumes an audience of fools. The wise counsel of the American people consists of their appearance in the crowd scenes staged for the cameras following the senator's balloons from the seacoasts of Maine to the old railroad towns in the Midwest.

"Giving all and risking all."
What Dole gives is the $60 million provided to his campaign at the taxpayers' expense. What he risks is nothing. By the second week in May his presidential campaign had been given up for dead. A Gallup poll conducted during the week of April 9 discovered 49 percent of the respondents saying that under no conceivable circumstance ("no chance whatsoever") would they vote for Dole. The Republican National Committee had begun to think of Dole as a liability (likely to harm the chances of every other Republican standing for election in November), and the Washington newspaper columnists seconded the motion of the gossip on Manhattan's Upper East Side—that Dole was a man who couldn't possibly be mistaken for a celebrity, a dreary orator and an uncomfortable presence on television, less interesting as a topic of conversation than one of the late John F. Kennedy's golf clubs, so inept at the art of image management that he delivered his first speech of the commencement season to a college for the deaf.

"As summer nears, and as the campaign begins, my heart is buoyant. Thank you, and may God guide us to what is right."
The buoyant heart is as improbable as the rest of the speech. By nature a cautious and sardonic man who introduced himself to a Florida political

rally by saying, "I'll be brief, since I know you have better things to do," Dole instinctively shuns the bright light and open spaces in favor of the side door, the back room, and the damp cellar. A merciful God would hide him from the sun at noon. But it is not God to whom the senator prays. He has made his deal with Mammon, and because Mammon drives as hard a bargain as Philip Morris or Chiquita banana, Dole stands blinking in the light like a ten-year-old girl making her debut on the grammar-school stage—dressed up in a spangled tutu, under instructions to smile and dance.

July 1996

Lights, Camera, Democracy!

> The poor have been rebels but they never have been
> anarchists; they have more interest than anyone else in
> there being some decent government; the poor man really
> has a stake in the country. The rich man hasn't; he can go
> away to New Guinea in a yacht. The poor have sometimes
> objected to being governed badly; the rich have always
> objected to being governed at all.
> —G. K. CHESTERTON

Well before the first rain of balloons fell on either of the summer's nominating conventions, it was hard to find a public-spirited citizen anywhere in New York who wasn't dissatisfied with the prospect of the November presidential election. No matter what the venue of the conversation—an editorial in the *New York Post,* a scholarly conference at NYU, a cocktail reception on Central Park West—the standard complaint relied on one or all of the following points:

1) Both candidates were paltry politicians.
2) Nobody was seriously discussing the serious issues.
3) The amoral news media subvert the hope of reason.
4) The country was being asked to vote for television commercials.

The dismal observations have become by now as much a matter of polite convention as remarks about the weather, and having listened to the requiem at the tomb of American politics for at least twenty years, I know when to regret the passing of Teddy Roosevelt, when to mention other crimes against democracy that the speaker might have overlooked, when to stare wistfully off into the historical past or glance sadly down at the marinated shrimp. But this year I ran across a more irritable tone in the voices of mourning, and on the Monday before the Fourth of July I was taken unawares by a sudden silence at a dinner party on East Sixty-fourth Street. Apparently I had missed one of the antiphonal responses, and both the woman on my left (a partner at Salomon Brothers) and the man sitting opposite (a network television correspondent) were waiting for my contribution to the sum of the nation's sorrow. I couldn't remember whether they had been finding fault with the Unabomber or Senator Alfonse D'Amato, but on the assumption that what was wanted was something politely apocalyptic, I said that if things kept going the way they were going, then we might as well assign the management of the country's politics to the Disney Company. The woman frowned, and the man impatiently tapped the table with his salad fork. They reminded me that we were talking about the most awesome office in the free world, about the fate of nations and the destiny of mankind, and that the topic was not one that invited levity. Anxious to avoid another mistake, I listened to the rest of the evening's conversation a good deal more closely than usual, wondering why the company was so skittish.

To most of the forty-odd people in the room—among them two or three Wall Street lawyers, several journalists, a Washington lobbyist, a television producer in town from Los Angeles, at least four investment bankers, the owner of a recently formed company supplying racetrack results on the Internet, and the proprietor of a resort island off the coast of North Carolina—the result of the November election was a matter of little consequence. Both candidates were as sound as J. P. Morgan or Ronald Reagan in their belief that money was good for the rich and bad for the poor, and what else was it important to know? Most everybody present was in the business of managing the world's traffic in expensive images—rendered as Hollywood movies and programs of political reform as well as stock-market symbols and Italian silk—and because the traffic was international, they found themselves more at ease with their economic peers in London, or Tokyo, or Berlin, than with their poorer fellow citizens encountered, preferably at a safe distance, in the streets of Miami or Chicago.

Nor were most of the guests much interested in the mechanics (as opposed to the theatrics) of American politics or much worried about the future prospects of the American commonwealth. It was a fairly safe guess that few of them could name their congressman or deputy mayor and an even-money bet that several of them had shifted their principal financial assets to Switzerland or Grand Cayman. They could afford to think that the difference between a Republican and Democratic administration was the difference between a marginally higher or lower tax rate and the number of invitations likely to be extended by the organizers of Washington policy conferences. Were Dole to be elected, the banker seated under the Picasso drawing might become a cabinet official; if Clinton remained in office, the television producer might be appointed to a presidential commission meant to study (and be appalled by) the quality of American education; in either event, one or two of the journalists might find themselves transformed into deputy secretaries of state. Otherwise the election would come and go without noticeable effect, the summer's campaign rhetoric as promptly forgotten as Newt Gingrich's Contract with America or the evening's carrot soup.

Why then the attitudes of grave foreboding? Why not simply enjoy the comedy of the nominating conventions and take comfort in the accumulating profits in the stock market? The questions stayed in mind during the somber discussions of Clinton's failures as a statesman and Dole's failures as an actor, and by the time the caterers served the lemon sorbet I understood that the criticisms of the year's political entertainment encompassed two sets of concerns, one of them about the style of the performance, and the other, more troublesome but less clearly expressed, about its lack of meaning. Although few of the people at dinner believed in the practice of democratic self-government, they deemed the belief necessary to the maintenance of public order. Too general a loss of faith in the symbols of democracy might lead to rioting in the streets, and it was therefore incumbent upon the managers of Democracyland to make a good show of flags and speeches and counting votes. But the guests also wished to think of themselves as patriots instead of exiles; worried about their own degrees of separation from what was once a familiar plot, they were reluctant to concede that the American political system grants parallel sovereignty to both a permanent and a provisional government, and that it is always a mistake to let them be seen as different entities.

The permanent government, a secular oligarchy of which the company at dinner was representative, comprises the *Fortune* 500 companies and their attendant lobbyists, the big media and entertainment syndicates, the civil and military services, the large research universities and law firms. It is this government that hires the country's politicians and sets the terms and conditions under which the country's citizens can exercise their right—God-given but increasingly expensive—to life, liberty, and the pursuit of happiness. Obedient to the rule of men, not laws, the permanent government oversees the production of wealth, builds cities, manufactures goods, raises capital, fixes prices, shapes the landscape, and reserves the right to assume debt, poison rivers, cheat the customers, receive the gifts of federal subsidy, and speak to the American people in the language of low motive and base emotion.

The provisional government is the spiritual democracy that comes and goes on the trend of a political season and oversees the production of pageants. It exemplifies the nation's moral aspirations, protects the citizenry from unworthy or unholy desires, and devotes itself to the mending of the American soul. The tribunes of the people mount the hustings to give voice to as many of the nation's conflicting ideals as can be recruited under the banners of freedom and fitted into the time allowed, ideals so at odds with one another that the American creed rests on the rock of contradiction—a self-righteously Christian country that supports the world's largest market for pornography and cocaine; a nation of prophets and real estate developers that defines the wilderness as both spiritual retreat and cash advance; the pacifist outcries against the evils of the weapons industry offset by the patriotic demand for an invincible army; a land of rugged individualists quick to seek the safety of decision by committee.

Positing a rule of laws instead of men, the provisional government must live within the cage of high-minded principle, addressing its remarks to the imaginary figure known as the informed citizen or the thinking man, a superior being who detests superficial reasoning and quack remedies, never looks at *Playboy,* remembers the lessons of history, trusts Bill Moyers, worries about political repression in Liberia, reads (and knows himself improved by) the op-ed page of the *Wall Street Journal.*

When giving voice to one or another of the conflicting ideals at large among the population, the provisional government—as liberal as it is conservative, enthusiastically welcoming ideas from both the Republican and Democratic workshops of liberty—promotes heroic public works projects as hopelessly incapable of construction as the flat tax, the balanced budget, the Republican Revolution, or Clinton's reform of the health care system. It is the provisional government that demands the breaking off of trade with China (on the ground that the Chinese shoot political prisoners and make copies of Tom Cruise movies); it is the permanent government that ignores the demand on the ground that too many American manufacturers have become dependent on cheap Chinese labor. The provisional government proposes a constitutional amendment to make abortion a crime against the state; the permanent government discounts the proposal as both foolish and impractical. The provisional government passes mandates for racial preference and affirmative action; the permanent government hires whom it chooses to hire. The provisional government undertakes to guarantee health insurance to every family in America; the permanent government decides the gesture is too expensive.

The multiplication of good intentions lends verisimilitude to the morality play about a democratic republic delighting in the joys of free expression. But let the words threaten to result in actions that will disturb the comfort of the permanent government and the speaker quickly comes to be seen as a dangerous and irresponsible demagogue. While the snow was still on the ground during last winter's primary campaigns in Ohio and New Hampshire, Patrick J. Buchanan's vivid rhetoric was perceived as harmless entertainment. He was fun to have around, and to hear him talk about stoning abortionists and gunning down peasants on the Mexican border was like reading a book about Genghis Khan. By the third week in March it had occurred to all concerned (to the news media as well as to the political establishment in North Carolina) that an embarrassing number of voters might take Buchanan at his word, and his candidacy melted away in the first warmth of spring.

The genius of elected politicians consists in their ability to sustain the pretense that the two governments are one and the same while simultaneously satisfying the very different expectations of their temporal and spiritual constituencies. The effort calls for a sense of occasion. When standing in the well of the Senate or when seated in a television studio opposite Tom Brokaw, it is the duty of politicians to denounce sin and read from the American book of virtues, to insist that the drug traffic be stopped, Saddam Hussein punished, and the federal budget brought into balance. Offstage, and between appearances on C-SPAN, it is the duty of politicians to arrange, in the manner of bootleggers during Prohibition, steady supplies of subsidy and debt. Speaking to a national television audience on a Wednesday night in the spring of 1995, Dole presented himself as a member of the provisional government and waxed indignant about the immorality of Hollywood films that exhort honest and up-standing citizens to misplace their children and abandon their wives. A few days later, reconstituted as a member of the permanent government at a fund-raising dinner in Las Vegas that provided $477,450 to his presidential campaign, Dole assured the owners of that city's gambling casinos that he would scotch any misguided attempt on Capitol Hill to pass a law limiting their profits.

As with the different forms of polite language, so also with the different rules of proper conduct. Acts deemed praiseworthy when performed by agents of the permanent government (stealing trade secrets, rigging balance sheets, selling junk bonds) appear blasphemous or obscene when attempted (under the rubrics of foreign espionage and inventive fiscal policy) by the servants of the provisional government. IBM dismisses 125,000 superfluous workers, and the newsstands thicken with four-color praise for the happy return of the entrepreneurial spirit that made the country great. The Senate votes to eliminate 150,000 crippled chil-dren from the welfare rolls, and the sponsors of the bill stand accused of sadism. A stock market swindler sells a book of claptrap economic the-ory for a publisher's advance of $1 million, and he shines forth on the best-seller list as a friend of the common man. Newt Gingrich signs a similar deal for a similar book with Rupert Murdoch, and enraged Democrats recommend an ethics investigation. By confessing to the monstrosity of their sexual appetites, movie stars add luster to their celebrity; Senator Bob Packwood tells his diary about his bungling search for love in a harem of staff assistants and finds himself expelled from Congress.

The quadrennial presidential election is the most solemn of the festivals staged by the provisional government, and the prolonged series of cere-monies—the ceaseless round of public opinion polls, the muster of ear-nest newspaper editorials, the candidates riding the parade floats of the Washington talk shows—belong to the same order of events as the songs and dances performed at a Zuni corn harvest. The delegates gather to invest the next President of the United States with the magical prowess of a kachina doll, embodying the country's ancestral truths and meant to be exhibited in hotel ballrooms and baseball parks. Bustling with im-ages salvaged from the costume trunks of American history, the amplified voices of conscience ascend the pulpits of liberty to proclaim their faith in nobody knows exactly what, but something that has to do with a noble spirit, a just society, and America the Beautiful. As always, the language is abstract, the speakers being careful to avoid overly specific reference to campaign finance reform or the depletion of the Social Security trust fund (questions best left to the sounder judgment of the permanent government) and directing their passion to the telling of parables—about character, thrift, integrity, family values, individual initiative, points of light. The intention is to make a loud and joyful noise in which the contradictions inherent in the American creed will vanish in a cloud of balloons or march triumphantly out of the convention hall with one of the high school bands.

What troubled the company at dinner on East Sixty-fourth Street was the lack of *gravitas* in this year's staging of the America Is a Democracy Festival. Neither candidate took naturally to wearing the masks of bountiful renewal. Clinton was too obviously made of wax (i.e., a contrivance of the provisional government so often stamped with the faces of contradiction that it had lost all sense of identity), and the bright linen of his public virtue was noticeably soiled with the mud of scandal. Dole was too obviously a creature of the permanent government, the kind of man one wants to know at 4:00 a.m. in an after-hours club but not the next morning in church. The grotesque inadequacies of the two candidates offended the sophistication of the Manhattan dinner guests, all of them accustomed to seeing Pavarotti in *Tosca* and Michael Jordan in Madison Square Garden. Here they were in the front row of American success, and the stumbling performance of the prayer for rain was an insult to both their intelligence and wealth. The television correspondent mentioned the summer's competing attractions, among them the Olympic Games in Atlanta, and asked indignantly why, if America was still the richest and most powerful country on earth, it couldn't stage a better minstrel show.

Other voices at other tables extended the range of complaint to the lack of principled people in Washington and the loss of civility in the films of Oliver Stone. The unanimous tone of nervous irritation suggested that the guests had begun to worry about what might happen to their own privileged estate if it became too apparent that the agendas of the permanent and provisional governments had as little to do with each other as the bond market and the phases of the moon. Over the last four or five years, entirely too many people (envious and irresponsible people) had been talking about the widening gulf between the fortunes of the rich and the misfortunes of the poor. The fact was certainly plain enough, but what if it should become too widely accepted as proof that the premise of an egalitarian democracy was as extinct as the Dusky Seaside Sparrow?[1]

The company at dinner had noticed that something was amiss in the engine room of freedom. They could tell by looking at the crowds in the streets, and by the airport and restaurant signs they saw printed in Korean or Spanish, that the United States was tending toward the multiracial and multilingual society described by literary academics as antidemocratic and portrayed on advertising posters as the United Colors of Benetton. The newly enfiefed minorities might respect the same rules of commercial enterprise, but who was to say that they would agree to belong to the same political enterprise? Anybody could open a grocery store or operate a fleet of taxicabs, but it was something else entirely to know the words of the Marine Hymn and the "Ballad of Buffalo Bill." The division of the country into separate provinces of feeling (some of them as large as Louis Farrakhan's Nation of Islam, others as militant as the Freemen lately confined to quarters in Jordan, Montana) made it increasingly difficult to bind together what was once the American polity with a common narrative. It was getting harder and harder to pump up the parade balloons with the willing suspensions of disbelief, which was why the news media were sending 15,000 correspondents of various magnitudes to the summer nominating conventions, why the networks already had granted free time to both candidates in October, why the campaigning season never ends. If the American Commonwealth was nowhere to be found among the strip malls between Boston and San Diego (a wilderness in which the squares of safe suburban lawns begin to seem as isolated from one another as the fortified stockades on

---

1   The standard set of observations attributes the increasing distances between rich and poor to the policies of the Reagan and Bush Administrations, but the trend has become even more evident under the auspices of the Clinton Administration. Supported in large part by the steady rise in the stock market (up 61 percent in the last three years), the share of the nation's income going to the wealthiest 5 percent of the population increased from 18.6 percent to 20 percent in 1993 to 21.1 percent in 1994. Within the last eighteen months, roughly 1 million men between the ages of twenty-five and fifty-five (i.e., in their prime working years) disappeared from the labor force.

the old Western frontier) maybe it could be simulated on television—not only with the convention broadcasts and the pious commentary of David Brinkley but also in the exemplary displays of egalitarian good fellowship presented by *Seinfeld* and *Murphy Brown*.

Reminded of the media's ceaseless advertisement for a democratic reality, I understood that the evening's lament was also part of the necessary ritual. The guests might as well have been shaking cornstalks and beating feathered drums. As statements of fact, none of the points of complaint about the November election made any sense. Few of the people present had any use for politicians who weren't paltry, for the perfectly good reason that non-paltry politicians disturbed the status quo. Nor did they wish to engage in serious discussion of any issues that might seriously inhibit the sovereignty of money. The country was being asked to vote for television commercials because only in the happy, far-off land of television commercials could the American democracy still be seen to exist. But understood as ritual chant, the remarks at dinner sustained the nostalgic remembrance of time past. The company might object, in Chesterton's phrase, "to being governed at all," but nobody was eager to sail away, at least not yet, to New Guinea or Barbados on a yacht, and if the political small talk was more obsessive than in years past, louder in volume and grimmer in tone, possibly it was because the citizens on East Sixty-fourth Street—as superstitious as the new media they habitually reviled and as stateless as the oligarchy of which they were a part—were making the noises of democracy to ward off the fell spirit of a future to which they couldn't give an American name.

August 1996

Back to School

Ambition hath no mean, it is either
upon all fours or upon tiptoes.
—Marquis of Halifax

*I*n early July I noticed a story in the *New York Times* about college professors at Amherst and Wesleyan dressing up their lecture courses with titles meant to draw a crowd—"Great Hits of Medieval Literature," "The Souls of Animals," "For Every Pharaoh There Is a Moses"—and I cut the page from the paper with the thought of writing an essay about the classical curriculum fitted to the wheel of progress and pressed into the mold of commercial trend. Two days later, before I had assembled even the beginning of an idea, I received a letter from H. J. Whitaker, a professor of English at a university in southern New England whom I had presumed safely immured in the research for his long-promised book on the Earl of Oxford. His letter rendered superfluous any commentary that I might have had in mind, but as with most of the news these days from the academic frontiers it requires a word of introduction.

Not having seen or heard from Whitaker in three years, I remembered him as a gray and bookish man obsessively preoccupied with the spectacle of the sixteenth century, a scholar fond of footnotes, lutes, and puns. But I also knew that he possessed an antic sense of humor, much refined by his study of the Elizabethan wits, and that if his circumstances had been somewhat different, he might have found his way onto the stage of *Saturday Night Live*. Apparently it was his gift for comedy that got him into trouble. When the chairman of the History Department fell suddenly ill last winter, Whitaker was asked to provide a spring-semester course that satisfied the requirements in both the history and humanities majors. "Nothing difficult," he said in his letter. "Nothing more than a few lectures sufficient to amuse the graduating seniors during their final season under the elm trees and to furnish the slow-witted among them with the last of their necessary credits."

The department didn't care what he taught, and because he happened to be re-reading Castiglione's *Book of the Courtier*, the principal Renaissance treatise on the staging of self-promotions, it occurred to him to teach the dance of grace and favor as performed by the ladies and gentlemen attending the magnificence of Lorenzo de' Medici and Elizabeth I. He had noticed that his students spent much of their time making connections and networking their address books ("grooming their résumés like show dogs"), and he thought they might enjoy knowing that their anxieties were as old as Hampton Court.

The dean objected to the proposition on the ground that it lacked "relevance," and before Whitaker knew what he was saying and without taking thought of the consequences, he shifted his *mise en scène* to the contemporary United States and set off on a manic improvisation aping and commenting upon the abject displays of flattery practiced not only by Washington politicians but also by the New York literary crowd, the grandees of the country's larger business corporations, and the hangers-on thriving like California mushrooms in the shadow of Steven Spielberg or Sharon Stone.

The dean was enchanted. Whitaker tried to disavow the performance, explaining that he had never met Spielberg or Stone (let alone Hillary Clinton or Salman Rushdie) and that he knew a good deal more about Shakespeare's Globe Theater than he did about Hollywood restaurants or the game of musical chairs in the executive offices of IBM and Time Warner. But the dean, a literal-minded man and desperate for enrollment, was already on the phone with the registrar.

"Never attempt a joke in the presence of a college administrator," Whitaker said. "Not unless it results in a gift to the library."

Attendance bore out the dean's sense of the market, and by the third week in April the classroom had become so crowded that late-arriving students were forced to stand in the hall or look in through the mullioned windows. The provost dropped by for the lecture on "The Trap of Friendship," which impressed him as a proof of the university's "commitment to the cutting edge of the twenty-first century," and on the Monday after Commencement the dean ordered Whitaker to prepare a full-year course under the title "The American Courtier: The Great Tradition." Offering the use of the Law School auditorium and the services of four research assistants, the dean clapped Whitaker on the back and told him that he was on his way to the academic limelight.

Whitaker didn't know whether he welcomed or dreaded the prospect. Although pleased by his new-found glory, he was nervous about both the size of the audience (the dean had mentioned upwards of 300 students) and the nature of the instruction (vocational instead of avocational), and because he was a diligent scholar, he knew that he hadn't done enough reading. The standard texts were obvious enough—Castiglione, La Bruyère's *Characters,* Saint-Simon's memoirs, Oscar Wilde's plays and aphorisms—but as he began searching the American sources he was astonished to discover that the Americans were even more assiduous than the Renaissance Italians in their cultivation of the garden of welcome lies. The literature was vast, in periodicals as well as books, consisting of self-help manuals, White House memoirs, celebrity confessions, and muckraking journalism, and the historical precedents were as unmistakable as the Washington Monument.

"Consider closely the lives of our great men," Whitaker said, "and who do we find beneath the surfaces of noble marble? True and worthy ancestors of our own beloved Bill Moyers and Barbara Walters."

Reading about the rules of self-advancement in Philadelphia in 1763, Whitaker had found Benjamin Franklin courting the favor of influential patrons, striking the pose of "the Humble Enquirer," preaching the virtues of calculation and civility, even writing verses in praise of caution, prudence, and coldness of heart—e.g., "The weakest Foe boasts some revenging Pow'r; The weakest Friend some serviceable Hour."

On the western frontier in 1831 Whitaker came across Alexis de Tocqueville passing through Nashville and Cincinnati and noticing that although the Americans didn't dress as well or as expensively as the ladies and gentlemen in France, they possessed a native talent for ingratiating themselves with anybody and everybody who could do them a service or grant them a privilege. Dandies in broadcloth instead of silk brocade, Whitaker said, loud in their brag and fantastic in their gestures, bowing and scraping in front of one another while standing up to their ankles in the muddy street of a wooden town.

But nothing had taken Whitaker more by surprise than the Horatio

Alger stories. "I had expected street urchins rising from rags to riches by dint of their hard work and noble character. Not at all. The Tattered Toms and Ragged Dicks succeed because they happen to be standing in the right place at the right time, encountering by accident a benign plutocrat for whom they play the part of dutiful and obliging son and so inherit the fortune."

Overwhelmed by the surfeit of sources, and knowing that he couldn't master all the variants of his topic within the time at hand, Whitaker still hoped to avoid making a fool of himself (especially if the child of somebody famous chanced to be sitting in the third row), and his apprehension brought him to the purpose of his letter. Enclosing the outline of lectures for the fall term, together with the synopsis that he had written for the college catalogue, he asked me to make any revisions that came to mind and encouraged me to show the syllabus to anybody else who might suggest improvements. I take the sentence to mean that he wouldn't mind seeing some of its finer passages in print.

CATALOGUE COPY

History 420: THE AMERICAN COURTIER
An examination of the means of personal self-advancement from the American Revolution to the present. Particular emphasis on the degrees of calculation necessary for a successful career in business, politics, or the arts.

Prerequisite: History 121 or the equivalent. Readings in Castiglione, Shakespeare, Saint-Simon, Talleyrand, Franklin, Wilde, Kissinger, Bradlee, Clinton, Liz Smith.
MWF/1:30–2:20 Cr/year only

COURSE OF STUDY FALL TERM

Week 1—The Courtier as the Hero of Our Time
1) Discarding negative stereotypes and correcting false impressions.
2) The courtier not to be confused with the toady, the suck-up, the lick-spittle, or the brown-nose (Castiglione, Diderot, Bob Woodward, Larry King).
3) Prostitution an honorable profession (Selected readings: the *Wall Street Journal*'s editorial page).

Week 3—Opinions
1) The safety of platitudes: candor always a mistake.
2) Successful topics of conversation—sports, birds, foreigners, gardens, movie stars, zoos, money.
3) Ignorance a blessing; fitting an opinion to the color of the drapes; the art of saying absolutely nothing *(Foreign Affairs, The American Spectator)*.

Week 6—Striking Poses
1) The importance of being seen, especially in the company of people more celebrated than oneself *(People,* assorted gossip columnists).
2) Politics compared to fashion photography; the poses of Senator Alfonse D'Amato likened to those of Cindy Crawford.
3) Which books and moral certainties to bring to literary conferences; whether to play tennis or go on the rafting trip; learning to think of oneself as an expensive suit.

Week 9—Flattery
1) Why there never can be too much of it (biographies of Lee Iacocca and Alexander Haig).
2) The seven degrees of the servile smile (videotape, ABC News—Jennings, Donaldson, Walters).
3) Fulsome compliments and congratulatory notes (the collected letters of Bill Clinton and George Bush).

Week 10—The Trap of Friendship
1) A friend a foolish luxury. Loyalty not a virtue.
2) The distinction between a friend and a connection. The glance sinister and the cut direct.
3) The timely betrayal (Kissinger, Nixon, et al.).

Week 12—Appearances, Their Sovereign Rule
1) It is only shallow people who do not judge by appearances. Knowledge differentiated from knowingness. Showing credibility and resolve.
2) Perception management; cosmetic surgery; shoes and hats.
3) The perfect courtier (Colin Powell, Diane Sawyer).

On reading Whitaker's notes for the second time, I could see him warming to his theme, persuaded of its seriousness by the force of his own rhetoric, and I wondered why Yale and Harvard hadn't thought to offer

a similar course of study. Certainly the character of the unctuous careerist was as familiar in faculty common rooms as in Washington policy
institutes and Hollywood television studios, and why not present the
character as an admirable one? Why not, in Whitaker's phrase, "put an
end to the old Puritan superstitions about the wickedness of silk and
Charles II"?

Caught up in the excitement of transferring his preoccupation with
Elizabethan etiquette to the protocols of late-twentieth-century American wealth and celebrity, Whitaker was offended by our own latter-day
media, "both news and entertainment divisions," continuing the program of moralizing sermons about the American hero as a voice of
conscience, forever crying in the wilderness, standing on a principled
soapbox to announce, usually to a crowd of seven, a bitter or eternal
truth. "What rot!" he said. "The pieties ignore the facts." What else is
the courtier spirit, he said, if not the spirit of a society overrun by
lawyers? A lawyer, like any journalist or actor, is by definition a courtier
hired to arrange the truth in its most flattering and convenient poses, a
smiling and accommodating person loyal to power under whatever name
it presents itself, constructing the edifice of a brilliant career by saying
to a succession of masters: Make of me what you want; I am what you
want me to be.

Roused to the point of righteous indignation, Whitaker asked a
prosecutor's question: "Isn't this the attitude that corporations expect of
their junior executives, or campaign managers of their candidates, or
women of their dogs?" His studies had convinced him that the courtier
spirit is far more necessary to a democracy than to a monarchy. The
figure of the prince wears so many faces (network executive, town clerk,
syndicated columnist) that a democracy transforms the relatively few
favors in a monarch's gift (sinecure, benefice, patents royal) into the vast
supply of grace and favor distributed under the rubrics of tax exemption,
defense contract, publication, milk subsidy, tenure. Courts form like
oyster shells not only around the pearls of great price at IBM and the
Walt Disney Company but also around Oprah Winfrey and Wayne
Gretzky. Once instructed in the correct forms of agreeable behavior and
expedient speech, the ambitious careerist in attendance at one court
finds it a simple matter to perform the same services for other well-
placed patrons in other well-furnished rooms.

Which presumably is why Whitaker's dean booked him into the Law
School auditorium. If the reports in the newspapers can be believed,

college students these days worry about missing the last train to Greenwich, Connecticut, or the golden beaches of Florida and California. Well aware that they have little choice but to become dependent upon a corporate overlord (not only for wages but for the terms of their existence, for pension, medical insurance, club membership, and definition of self), how could they not want to learn the ways and means of keeping their places in the sun? Another three semesters in the academic limelight, and I can imagine Whitaker, sometimes on tiptoes but more often on all fours, addressing business conventions, developing projects for PBS, lecturing at the Kennedy School of Government.

September 1996

Oklahoma Lobster

September 4, 1996

Dominion Research Associates
13150 Lee Highway
Fairfax, Virginia 22033

T. Preston Redpath
Committee to Re-elect the President
Jefferson Hotel
1200 16th Street N.W.
Washington, D.C. 20036

Dear Ted,

In answer to your first question, our polling data show that the President's decision to sign the welfare bill was undoubtedly the correct one and that you have no cause to worry about a significant number of voters giving way in October to any late upsurge of compassion. Ever since the disappearance of TWA Flight 800 to Paris, and the bombing in Atlanta ten days later, all the instruments of measurement—focus group, telephone survey, printed questionnaire—indicate broad consensus (by margins of 40 percent) on the following points:

1) Fear is bipartisan.
2) When in doubt, restrict access and tighten security.
3) You can never have enough police.

Congress had the good sense to pass the welfare bill while the wreck-age of the TWA plane was still being fished out of the ocean off eastern Long Island, and the news media didn't need to be told which was the better story. Neither did most of the politicians up for election this fall. Instead of talking about the cruelty of the revised social contract be-tween the American people and their government, they chased one an-other around the circle of photo opportunities, demanding the swift punishment of foreign terrorists. But foreign terrorists are hard to locate, much less line up against the wall of justice. Fortunately for the Presi-dent's prospects in November, our data suggest a blurring in the public mind of the distinction between poverty and crime. Ronald Reagan made the two words into synonyms, and the respondents in the richer zip codes (i.e., the people likely to vote) tend to associate Arabs carrying suitcases of plastique explosives with illegal Mexican immigrants carry-ing rakes and hoes, also with unmarried mothers carrying babies. The wish to punish foreign thugs comes naturally to rest on the domestic poor, who are easier to find. Most of them are children.

Your second question—how to stay ahead of, or at least keep pace with, the conservative trend in the country—is more interesting. Be-cause statistical analysis never provides sufficient context, I spent most of August canvassing the vanguard of reactionary opinion assembled at weekend conferences by various political and religious organizations devoted to the reclamation of America the Beautiful and America the Good. At the meetings in Dallas and Orlando, the congregants fit the description of the delegates to the Republican Convention in San Di-ego—middle-aged white men, many of them wealthy but most of them so besotted with platitudes that I didn't learn anything useful. The more instructive conference, at which I registered as a systems manager from Palo Alto, took place at a Sheraton hotel near Valley Forge. I hadn't thought that the tide of ideological rancor had come so far east and north, or that the delegates would prove to be so young. I must have talked to twenty or thirty people who looked like Congressman John Kasich or Ralph Reed—neatly dressed, polite, equipped with laptop computers and cellular phones, smiling the enraptured smiles of newly commissioned ensigns aboard the Starship *Enterprise*. When they spoke of the bright reawakening of American prosperity certain to follow from the passage of the welfare bill (or from the constitutional amendments forbidding abortion and reviving the practice of school prayer), their enthusiasm was genuine, the product of steadfast and long-abiding ignorance rather than a matter of expedient maneuver.

At the banquet on Saturday night (in the interval between the songs by Donny Osmond and the speech by Oliver North) the conversation at table 17 turned to the always congenial topic of crime and punishment, and all present agreed that the United States tolerated entirely too much of the former and proscribed not nearly enough of the latter. In an attempt to lighten the proceedings, I foolishly attempted a sardonic joke. You would have known better, Ted. You would have told me that our literal-minded friends from the leafy suburbs don't have much of an ear for satire. It was a shame, I said, that in these decadent times we have lost the fine old medieval customs of public execution and torture. The remark was greeted with nods of approval, and before the weekend was over six delegates asked me for further information, wanting to know what books they could trust to provide them with reliable histories of the fourteenth century. What was instructive was the stature of the people taking notes—a lobbyist for The Citizens Union, a program officer from the F. W. Olin Foundation, one of William Bennett's research assistants, an executive in the upper ranks of the Coors Brewing Company. Their interest was heartfelt, and their follow-up questions constitute the lesson of Valley Forge.

To judge the possible relevance of the lesson to the President's election campaign, you should know that I told the company at dinner that during the late Middle Ages the leading cities and towns in western Christendom bid against one another for the right to execute criminals condemned to death by either the civil or the canon law. Members of the nobility and senior clergy ordinarily sold for higher sums than peasants, but the market price depended on the regional demand for moral lessons and cautionary tales, which, by the accounts of both Barbara Tuchman and Johan Huizinga, was always pressing. If the townspeople of Bruges were showing signs of heresy and discontent, slow to pay their rents, neglecting their family values, abandoning themselves to sorcery and drink, the municipal authorities might pay a premium—100 florins more than Ghent—for the chance to draw and quarter an obscure but lecherous monk. The market also accommodated itself to the particular talents of a town's resident executioner. If Bologne boasted the presence of a man so skilled in the art of torture that he could prolong the prisoner's death through the whole of an afternoon, the town might pay 200 ducats more than Calais for a woodcutter sturdy enough to bear an extended siege of pain. In other words, as I explained to the guests at table 17, the medieval market in live criminals was as steady as our own market for live lobsters. The trade didn't depend on the capture of occasional celebrities (i.e., individuals as notorious as the Unabomber), and if the local executioner knew what he was about, he could evoke an image of God's wrath on the undernourished body of a ten-year-old child as well as on the rosy flesh of a well-fed cardinal or duke. Huizinga mentions four blind beggars armed with knives and made to fight for a pig, also the execution of several robbers that excited "a great deal of laughter because they were all poor men."

The Coors executive was the quickest to grasp the commercial possibilities. Because his corporation was accustomed to financing right-wing academic studies that deplored the malignant growth of the country's criminal enterprise, he had the figures readily available: 1.5 million inmates in American prisons, another 3.5 million suspicious persons on probation or parole, over 3,000 condemned prisoners awaiting execution on one or another of the country's death rows. Furiously computing the numbers on his pocket calculator, he marveled at the abundance of a natural resource as open to the improving hand of progress as the nineteenth-century Colorado wilderness before the coming of the railroad. Now, as then, the profit in the business would accrue to the man who had the wit to foster a market for his goods, and the Coors executive projected a heavy demand for what he called, with a sly wink and a big grin, "our Oklahoma lobster." He reminded me that all across America the cities and towns that had lost their means of livelihood to the higher technologies were so desperate for revenue that they welcomed the arrival of a prison or a toxic-waste dump. What would such a town not pay for the license to host tourist attractions bloodier than automobile races and more festive than golf tournaments? Transferring his numbers into a computer program (television rights, advertising sales, foreign distributions, bubble-gum cards), the Coors executive arrived at the vision of an annual draft ("similar to the ones conducted by the NFL or the NBA") at which different towns recruited prospects for the next year's sport. Although I didn't like to interrupt the flow of his enthusiasm, I pointed out that a draft probably wasn't a good idea, not because it didn't make perfect sense but because so many participants in the auction might too closely resemble the participants in the basketball auctions, and the liberal news media almost certainly would ring up the canard of racism.

Bill Bennett's research assistant, an attractive young woman who had studied comparative literature at both Harvard and the University of Virginia, was interested in the problem of rhetoric. How does one teach *The Book of Virtues* to people who can't read? Fine words have their uses, but they also have their limits. Nobody speaks more plainly about the corrosive viciousness of network television than Bill Bennett, or writes more cogently than Charles Murray about the futility of affirmative action, but to what purpose their eloquence? Who listens to them? Their words sink into either the trash heap of the tabloid press, and it is as if nothing has been said. The newspapers the next day report a new round of murders in Brooklyn, and another nightclub singer or former FBI agent steps up to a microphone to give evidence of Bill Clinton's sexual crimes.

Four or five years ago maybe it was enough to go to the movies and see Arnold Schwarzenegger kill fifty or sixty Arabs in the twinkling of an explosion, or watch Bruce Willis throw a German terrorist off the roof of a Los Angeles office building, but despite the box-office success of *Independence Day* (hordes of alien invaders destroyed in a triumph of Dolby sound) the cinematic homilies somehow had lost their moral force. The audience was too jaded, too familiar with the vocabulary of special effects, and probably the time had come to teach by example instead of precept. When one got to thinking about it, the young woman said, "I mean *really* thinking about it, in the way that Derrida or Foucault would have thought about it"—torture was a kind of language.

The man from the Olin Foundation also appreciated the need for cautionary tales (a need even more pressing in twentieth-century America than in fourteenth-century France), but his line of thought was less theoretical. He was concerned about the muttering of honest Americans obliged to submit to more stringent security measures, not only at airports but also in their homes and places of work. That such restrictions were necessary he didn't for a moment doubt—regrettable, of course, and not what one might have wished for the children of liberty, but clearly necessary in a world that allowed three fanatic Mohammedans to step out of a taxi in Cairo and shoot down eighteen Greek tourists in front of the Europa Hotel. The circumstances obviously warranted harsher enforcement of stricter rules—more wiretaps, earlier curfews, less noise, a healthy regimen of arbitrary arrests. But people didn't always take kindly to inconvenience, even in the interest of their own safety, and if the good citizens of Orange County were to be required to make sacrifices, they needed to see some results, "some pretty damn specific and impressive results."

Other conversations at Valley Forge pointed in the same authoritarian direction, a majority of the respondents saying that punishment is good for people, that it strengthens their character. If we also bear in mind the polls taken at the San Diego convention (the ones showing the Christian Coalition people in favor of the government assuming the prerogatives of a militant church), I think that we can safely conclude that the Dole campaign already has scheduled their candidate to make a cameo appearance at an execution in Alabama sometime in late October. Dole's people worry that Jack Kemp's reputation as a dithering liberal might disappoint the evangelist wing of the party, and they will try to steady Dole's image as a man of high principle and firm resolve. To once again anticipate and forestall the Republicans, you should tell somebody in your shop to look through the prison calendar at Huntsville, Texas, and if we can find a criminal convicted of an especially repugnant crime (if possible, the murder of a child) we might consider sending the President to witness his punishment in the electric chair. The President needn't make a speech. He stands in the shadows and a little to one side, a stern and commanding figure from the pages of the Old Testament, come to see to it that justice is done. Although I know the President likes to occupy center stage, I don't think he should throw the switch. At least not this year. Maybe in the fullness of time, when opinion has shifted somewhat further to the right.

When I see you next week at Carol's dinner, we'll talk about the forthcoming debates and whether the summer was kind to your backhand.

Yours,
Chuck

October 1996

Painted Fire

Well, humor is the great thing, the saving thing, after all.
— MARK TWAIN

On the same afternoon in early September that Random House offered Dick Morris $2.5 million for yet another book applying yet another coat of mud to the character of President Bill Clinton, I ran across three New York editors in the lobby bar of the Algonquin Hotel who read in the announcement yet another reason to mourn the passing of H. L. Mencken. Sitting under the potted palms familiar in the 1930s to the Algonquin roundtable of celebrated wits (among them Harpo Marx and Dorothy Parker), and being literary people old enough to remember the world before television, they buttressed their remarks with invidious comparisons between time past and time present. Here was the braggart Morris, a rank opportunist newly famous for his adoration of a prostitute's toes, but where was the writer capable of skewering the fellow on the spit of satire? Where was Mencken? Where, for that matter, were Ambrose Bierce and Mark Twain? What had become of "our native genius for brutal sarcasm and savage wit"? The earth groaned under the weight of scoundrels and fools, but deliverance was nowhere at hand, or even in sight.

The three editors pursued the subject for the better part of an hour, ordering more gin and adding names to their list of books and authors deserving of death by ridicule, and by the time the waiter brought the third round of drinks, I was imagining Mencken miraculously risen from the grave, pushing through the doors of the hotel with a cigar in his

mouth and a manuscript under his arm. Like Bierce and Twain, the sage
of Baltimore was not known for his deference to the pieties of the age,
and I thought it probable that within a matter of a very few minutes, the
two ladies and one gentleman regretting his absence would find even
more pressing reasons to regret his presence. Some of Mencken's offhand
remarks came more or less readily to mind—his classification of Franklin D. Roosevelt as a demagogue of the same ilk as Mussolini, his description of Philadelphia as "an intellectual slum," his belief that even an
absolute and intransigent monarchy was "appreciably superior" to the
American system of democratic government, his contempt for the average man, his definition of the American politician, any American politician, as a man who crawls and "knows the taste of the boot-polish."
Except for the last remark (permissible only if pertaining to Morris or a
dead Nazi), few or none of Mencken's opinions would make themselves
welcome on the editorial page of the newspaper that the woman on my
right served as a leading liberal ornament, or on the fall list of the
publishing house that the gentleman on my left devoted to the manufacture of celebrity biographies, all or most of which could carry the uniform title *My Life on the B-List* or *All About Me.*

Off the record and among themselves, the editors in distress were free
to despise the manuscripts they ushered into the light of print; even to
mock the generally accepted notions of government and law, but in their
public personae as protectors of the nation's intellectual health and
moral safety, they could no more afford to publish Mencken than they
could afford to question the beauty of Maya Angelou's poems or fail to
give thanks for the benefactions of Cardinal O'Connor and Rupert Murdoch.

Their predicament prompted me to wonder about the uses of satire in a
society that appears to have lost its appetite for objection and dissent.
Like Mencken, Twain thought of humor, especially in its more violent
forms of invective and burlesque, as a weapon with which to attack pride
victorious and evil arrogant. He placed the ferocity of his wit at the
service of his conscience, pitting it against the "peacock shams" of the
established order. Harboring no goodwill for what he called the "colossal
humbug" of the world, he believed that "only laughter can blow it away
at a blast."

The laughter that both Twain and Mencken had in mind has been
remanded to smaller magazines and the comedy clubs very far from

Broadway. The marketing directors who make the rules of commercial publishing regard humor of any kind as so specialized a commodity that the chain bookstores make no distinction between the works of Voltaire and those of Garfield the cat; both authors appear under signs marked HUMOR in order that the prospective reader will be advised to approach them with caution. The words might not mean exactly what they say.

In the respectable newspapers most of the commentary about Morris's sexual behavior was as literal-minded as *The Celestine Prophecy* or a book about how to make a fortune in Florida real estate. Several columnists remembered that it was Morris who had cajoled President Clinton into espousing the cause of family values, but their ironies were mild and offered little proof of the "native genius for brutal sarcasm and savage wit." A number of other columnists submitted statements on behalf of women's rights and the sacrament of marriage, but nothing much was said about Morris turning his term of White House service into a handsomely illustrated slander of the President. The practice has become standard over the last thirty years and no longer invites scorn. The media were more impressed by Morris's appearance on two successive covers of *Time* magazine, which moved them to jealous speculations about his enhanced worth on the talk-show and lecture circuits.

Nor did the general run of discussion about the season's presidential campaign amount to much more than a querulous complaint about the tawdriness of the rhetoric and the lack of noble sentiment. Ted Koppel removed the *Nightline* cameras from the Republican Convention in San Diego because the proceedings failed to meet his standard of portentousness, and except for Russell Baker in the *New York Times,* the upscale columnists in the respectable newspapers, eschewing satire for the safer course of indignant viewing-with-alarm, managed to sound like upscale food and furniture critics forced to shop at a Wal-Mart in Brockton, Massachusetts. Instead of being offered antique oratory as finely worked as a Tiffany lamp (memorable phrases, eloquent debates in old wooden rotundas, the voice of William Jennings Bryan), they were being presented with freeze-dried sound bites meant to be dropped into boiling water on *Larry King Live.*

The criticisms seemed a trifle churlish and unfair. Both candidates were doing their patriotic best to supply the desired atmospheres of a lost golden age—Hillary Clinton evoking the memory of a nineteenth-century American village green; her husband waving from a train that once had carried Harry Truman east from St. Louis; Jack Kemp permit-

ting himself the wistful hope for a triumphant return to the gold standard; candidate Dole saying in his acceptance speech that "all things flow
from doing what is right ... only right conduct distinguishe[s] a great
nation from one that cannot rise above itself. It has never been otherwise.
..." But the media, like Queen Victoria, were not amused.

Mencken, on the other hand, would have vastly enjoyed the proud
display of hypocrisies. I could imagine him rummaging through the
histories of ancient Rome, the Renaissance papacy, and imperial Spain in
a comically fruitless search for proofs of the theorem that great nations
achieve their places in the world by doing what is right. And when he
had done with the chaste and righteous acts performed by such exem-
plars of Christian deportment as Cesare Borgia and Cardinal Richelieu
and Otto von Bismarck, I could imagine him coming at last to the
bathos of Vice President Al Gore and the weeping for Christopher
Reeve, mocking the rose-colored images of the American paradise
shaped by the milk-white hand of Providence, the citadel of virtue and
ark of innocence, a nation so favored by God and Pat Robertson that it
never killed a buffalo or a Cherokee Indian, never ran a gambling casino
or lynched a Negro or bribed a judge or elected a president as stupid as
Warren Harding. And because it had behaved itself so well (always
doing right, always dressed for church), it had become a land entirely
overgrown with honeysuckle, where the urban poor go quietly off to
reservations in Utah and nobody, not even Dick Morris, fornicates on
Sunday afternoons.

The satirist attempts the crime of arson, meaning to set a torch of words
(what Twain called "painted fire") to the hospitality tents of pompous
and self-righteous cant. The intention presupposes readers well enough
aware of their own hypocrisies to see the stone of truth hidden behind
the back of the easy and not-so-genial smile. The country has never
produced such readers in commercial quantity. Even if Mencken or
Twain were to receive the necessary permission from the editors in the
Algonquin bar, where is the audience likely to be heartened by the news
that a society based on cash and self-interest is not a society at all but a
state of war? Notwithstanding the slides shown at the political conventions in San Diego and Chicago (the ones about the nonviolent and
peace-loving people at play in the fields of the Lord), America is a
country in which the Goodyear blimp often returns from its pleasant
afternoon over the golf course riddled with bullet holes, a country in

which 135,000 children bring guns to school, where a doctor is more likely to be punished for overcharging a patient than for killing or maiming one, where the labor conditions in the California strawberry fields are as destructive of human health and well-being as the explosion on TWA Flight 800, only over a slightly longer period of time, where a gang of thieves in Brooklyn robs banks with a backhoe, and where, with the hair shorn from the head and beard of Ted Kaczynski, a Montana barber ties trout flies called "The Bomber." Satire is humor sent on a moral errand, but the book-buying public is more familiar with publicity tours.

As forms of literary address, we nearly always have preferred the sermon and the sales pitch, and we seldom have had much use or liking for the voices of dissent. Tom Paine made the mistake of extending his defense of human liberty into a philippic against the despotism of the Christian church, an impiety for which he was reviled as a heretic, scorned as a drunkard, and denied church burial in the country that he had done so much to set free from England. American society turned out to be profoundly conformist, suspicious of any idea that couldn't be yoked to the wheel of progress, deeply reverent in the presence of wealth. Wit was predictably disastrous, and the ambitious clerk or college man soon learned that in the troubled sea of worldly affairs one sinks by levity and rises by gravity. Success entailed the keeping up of sober appearances and never venturing an opinion likely to affront the Mr. Pecksniff who owned the feed store. By the end of the nineteenth century satire had been largely confined to its gentler expressions (the kind that didn't need to be kept out of the hands of children), and Twain was obliged to reserve his more acerbic observations for posthumous publication, in the meantime playing the part of the harmless clown. Edith Wharton left for Europe, Finley Peter Dunne put on the mask of Mr. Dooley, and Bierce walked off the set into the deserts of northern Mexico.

Briefly revived during the intermission between World Wars I and II, the satirical spirit showed to brilliant effect not only among the Algonquin wits but also in the writings of Don Marquis, James Thurber, Albert J. Nock, Dawn Powell, and Sinclair Lewis, but the moment didn't last. Following upon its victories in the Second World War, the United States found itself transformed into an imperial power, and the delusions of grandeur had their usual ill effect. The fear of nuclear annihilation inhibited any sudden or subversive movement of the literary imagination, and the glorious return to economic prosperity restored the statues of Mammon to their golden pedestals in the country's better department stores. The country's governing and possessing classes, admiring their new patents of omnipotence in the mirror of an increasingly jingoistic press, acquired the habit of taking themselves very, very seriously indeed. They didn't look with favor upon the kind of jokes that cast doubt on the guarantees of immortality and the promise of redemption, and within the remarkable short space of the same six or seven years that brought forth the McCarthy hearings, the decay of the American satirical spirit begins to show up in the pages of the national magazines, the change of tone as clearly marked as the edges of the Gulf Stream when seen from a height of 20,000 feet. Prior to 1955, the writing exhibits the characteristics of people willing to laugh at their own vanity and intolerance; after 1955 the writing turns heavy and solemn, the authors laboring under the weight of sententious political theory and gazing into the wells of Narcissus.

If before 1960 it was possible to define literature, politics, journalism, and the movies as separate provinces of expression, over the last forty-odd years they have been fused into the alloy of the entertainment media and made subjects of an empire ruled by television. The television audience prefers situation comedy to satire, situation comedy and maybe the kind of sarcasm (pointed, but not so pointed as to lose the market) that lends itself to gridiron dinners, Academy Awards ceremonies, and *Saturday Night Live*. And because the television audience wishes to include itself in the good life seen on the screen (traveling to Europe, choosing between the Mercedes and the Lexis, conversing with Heather Locklear), the class bias of American humor, which once favored the least fortunate members of society at the expense of their self-important overlords, reversed direction, and much of what now passes for merry witticism on *Seinfeld* or *The Late Show with David Letterman* (as well as in the writing of P. J. O'Rourke or Rush Limbaugh) plays on the anxieties endured by the most fortunate members of the society when confronted with apparitions from the lower depths—scary street persons, hostile waitresses, ugly dogs. Given the trend of the times, it is conceivable that Morris could show up on *Oprah,* wearing his cute sailor hat, presenting himself as a victim unjustly exploited by the yellow press, saying that not all prostitutes these days have hearts of gold.

I mentioned the possibility to the editorial committee assembled in the Algonquin bar, but they interpreted the suggestion as a marketing strategy instead of a sarcasm, and I knew that Mencken wasn't coming back to West Forty-fourth Street and that when Twain said that satire preserved men from being "shrivelled into sheep," it didn't occur to him that lamb's wool would come to be so much admired.

November 1996

Dies Irae

Our ignorance of history makes us vilify our own age.
—FLAUBERT

*A*lthough the twentieth century still has three years remaining on the game clock, the heralds of apocalypse already have swarmed onto the field waving the banners of destruction and blowing the trumpets of doom. Their lamentations have become louder and more all-encompassing ever since the cancellation of the Cold War forced the publishers of prophetic texts to announce, among other calamities, *The End of History, The Death of Intimacy, The End of Nature, The Death of Economics, The End of Science,* and *The Death of Meaning.*

The projections of impending disaster (social, economic, and environmental) come and go like clouds across the horizon of the new millennium, and as recently as last summer I thought I had seen or heard most of the latter-day variants on the biblical book of Revelation. But I had forgotten about the seven bowls of God's wrath stored in the minds of some of the unhappier prophets on the reactionary right, and I wasn't familiar with the shrill voice of Robert H. Bork. When President Ronald Reagan nominated him to a place on the Supreme Court in 1987, I remembered seeing enough of his testimony before the Senate Judiciary Committee to know that he was a vain and arrogant man, suspicious of democratic government and not very well informed on the subject of American history. But until I came across his new collection of dire pronouncements, published in September under the title *Slouching To-*

wards Gomorrah, I had failed to properly classify him among the sooth-sayers who yell at the traffic on West Forty-second Street, warning Nigerian cabdrivers and transvestite prostitutes against the coming of the Antichrist, or who walk back and forth in front of the Port Authority Bus Terminal with a hand-lettered sign posting the date and time of the end of the world.

Whether admitted into evidence as history or prophecy, *Slouching Towards Gomorrah* is very poor stuff, and were it to be considered on its merits as a book, it could be safely remanded to oblivion. But the book reached the best-seller list within three weeks of its publication, and it bears discussion because of the paranoid rage that wells up in each of its seventeen chapters and because when people as prominent as Judge Bork come looking for you with sheriffs and dogs, it's helpful to know, or at least to guess at, the reasons for their anger. The author narrowly missed appointment to the Supreme Court, often sits at Pat Robertson's right hand on the evangelical talk-show circuit, and enjoys the full faith and credit of the conservative and neoconservative intellectual estab-lishments. The jacket copy boasts endorsements from John Cardinal O'Connor ("a thesis that cannot be ignored"), from Ralph Reed, the executive director of the Christian Coalition ("a tour de force"), from Michael Novak ("may be the most important book of the '90s").

The praise is either reckless or dishonest. The judge doesn't write nearly as well as the Unabomber, and his jeremiad, which is both less intelligent and less original, relies on secondhand sources and borrowed texts rather than on his own thought and observation. He has seen almost nothing of which he writes, and his book reads like a collection of notes taken at a series of academic conferences addressed to the topics of American decline, attended by the columnists for *The Weekly Standard,* and paid for by the Mobil Oil Corporation. By substituting dogma and abstraction for coherent narrative and historical fact, the judge can imagine the wreck of American civilization, that once noble work of Christian conscience, having been caused by a small band of traitorous intellectuals who, on or about the same day that the Beatles first showed up in America, bludgeoned the security guards surrounding the nation's top disc jockeys, gained access to the control booths, destroyed the Perry Como records, and broadcast "All You Need Is Love" to thirty million teenagers, all of them ripe with sexual yearning, who heard the song on their portable radios and so began to dance, naked and tumescent and unashamed, on the grave of Ralph Waldo Emerson. Soon afterward barbarians sacked the universities; atrocious liberals seized the movie studios; feminists captured the churches; nihilists took over the national parks; culture died.

Speaking as one "who detests modern liberalism and all its works," Bork follows the medieval practice of identifying God's enemies by category instead of by name. The tenth-century chroniclers worrying about the Day of Judgment scheduled for the end of the first millennium also knew that time was short and that already the world was filling up with Satan's "constant associates and inseparable companions," quite a few of them disguised as pious abbots, proud barons, or rich merchants, who went from place to place in the company of "magicians, enchanters, diviners and wizards" on whom they relied for instruction in "every evil, error and wicked art." In like manner, Bork mentions "radical feminists," "activist homosexuals," "multiculturalists" consumed with "hatred" and "contempt for American civilization," "black extremists." To all of these ministers of malice Bork ascribes characteristics appropriate to the Beast of the Apocalypse—"intolerant, untruthful," "hedonistic," "venomous," "abusive," "violent," envious," "decadent," "degraded," "brutal," "mindless," "debased." The adjectives litter every page of Bork's manuscript like graffiti on a wall.

Were Bork writing about specific individuals, or if he had an informed and complicated sense of the temperament and history of the American people, he might be less inclined to smear his book with insults. But like the nervous monks in medieval Europe, the judge isn't interested in the realms of everyday experience in which anonymous and therefore unimportant human beings go about the daily chores of living and dying and paying the bills. He writes about the world that exists only in the kingdom of images, not about the substance of American society but about its reflection in the mirrors of the media—about the movies, television news, popular music, the chatter in the universities.

Appalled by what he sees, he provides a list of necessary corrections, among them the imposition of strict codes of censorship on "the obscene prose and pictures available on the Internet, motion pictures that are mere rhapsodies to violence, and the more degenerate lyrics of rap music." Misguided people might think censorship contrary to the spirit of the First Amendment, but the judge meets the possible objections by saying that censorship has acquired an undeservedly bad press, "not because it has been tried and found dangerous or oppressive but because

the ethos of modern liberalism has made any interference with the individual's self-gratification seem shamefully reactionary."

Similar methods of argument accompany each of Bork's recommenda-
tions for restructuring American society along the lines of a Puritan
theocracy. The principles of liberty and equality he finds "pernicious"
and "much harder to reverse than it is comfortable to think." Jefferson
and the other founders of the American republic, all of them fooled by
the sophisms of the eighteenth-century Enlightenment, made the mistake of thinking that if human beings were released on their own recognizance, they would choose the good, the true, and the beautiful instead
of the wicked, the false, and the degenerate. Bork knows better. Freedom
is nothing but trouble and "has brought us to this—an increasing
number of alienated, restless individuals, individuals without strong ties
to others, except in the pursuit of ever more degraded distractions and
sensations."

For their own good, and for the good of the Republic, the restless
individuals need to be rounded up like sheep or cattle, but they have
nobody to herd them because America's intellectuals have failed in their
moral duty and sold their souls to the damnable "left." Bork doesn't
know why, but he has his suspicions:

> Perhaps the movement to the left was due to a combination of the intellec-
> tuals' hostility to bourgeois society and their well-known tendency to ad-
> mire power and even brutality
>
> Some of our elites—professors, journalists, makers of motion pictures and
> television entertainment, et al.—delight in nihilism and destruction as
> much as do the random killers in our cities.

As hopelessly beside the point on questions of law and politics as on
those of spiritual and aesthetic interest, Bork thinks the business corporations play a negligible part in "shaping the culture," that the student
protests of the 1960s derived none of their energies from the Vietnam
War or the civil-rights movement, that the lower classes commit crimes
and make vulgar sexual displays because of what they see on television,
not because of the conditions in which they happen to live. So indomita-
ble is the author's ignorance, and so serene his faith in right-wing political doctrine, that he can describe the current Supreme Court as an "agent
of modern liberalism" and say that "today intellectual and moral attack
on the bourgeois state comes almost entirely from the left." The former

statement ignores the presence on the Court of Justices Scalia, O'Connor, Thomas, and Rehnquist; the latter statement discounts the rhetorical onslaught directed by the Republican Party over the last twenty-five years against the army of evil bureaucrats camped in Washington under the flags of "big government."

Finally at a loss to know what it is that he is trying to say (other than that the country has seen and heard entirely too much of "Robert Redford, Jane Fonda, Gore Vidal, and those of similar ilk"), Bork attributes the nation's sorrow to the worship of Mammon. It is "affluence" that is at fault. "Affluence" that encourages "boredom" and "hedonism." "Affluence" that leads to "consumerism" and "self-indulgence." The Americans may not have known it at the time, but they were better off in the good old days of the Great Depression, because "religion tends to be strongest when life is hard, and the same may be said of morality and law. A person whose main difficulty is not crop failure but video breakdown has less need of the consolations and promises of religion."

Alas, the plague of affluence "reappeared in the late 1940's" (the economic corollary of the country's military triumph in the Second World War), and "it has remained with us since," tempting the faithful with refrigerators and college educations, breeding liberals. "The rot is spreading," and unless the American conscience responds to the emergency with some very stern countermeasures, the country must forfeit its chance of a happy return to the heavenly kingdom that Bork identifies with "the better aspects of the 1950's."

Not that Bork expects the American public to summon up the necessary courage or force of will. Like the inhabitants of Gomorrah, we are too degenerate, too depraved. We have sunk too low into the swamp of "modern liberalism," wandered too far into the maze of "radical individualism," seen too many photographs of Madonna, read too many editorials in the *Washington Post*. We are all lost, all doomed to listen in Hell to the music of Snoop Doggy Dogg.

It wasn't as if we hadn't been told. Bork tried to tell us. So did James Q. Wilson and George Will and Gertrude Himmelfarb, all of them indexed in Bork's tract among his principal sources of information. But we failed to heed the warnings. We transgressed the laws, violated the statutes, and broke the everlasting covenants. Now that America lies polluted under its television antennae, the time has come to pay what Judge Bork hopes will prove to be a terrible price. Terrible but just.

The judge rejoices in the prospect of punishment, and he longs for the purifying fire of Armageddon, that great day foretold in the book of Revelation when the sea becomes like the blood of a dead man and the false prophets gnaw their tongues in anguish. The cry for vengeance sounds through the whole of judge Bork's bitter text. The mumble of violent adjectives serves as the ominous hanging of a ritual drum, and when the author feels obliged to say a few words about the good society (the one yoked to the plows of Christian virtue as opposed to the Sodom on the Potomac or the Gomorrah on the Hudson), he conceives it along the lines of a well-run prison.

But why is Bork so angry, Bork the loyal and well-remunerated servant of the corporate state, cosseted by the media that he so ungratefully reviles, Bork the sage of K Street, blessed by both the Christian Coalition and the National Chamber of Commerce? From what poisoned well does he draw the bile from which to cultivate the garden of his rage?

His intolerance comes trailing clouds of pride and envy, and on reading his book I thought of W. H. Auden's lines from the poem "September 1st, 1939": "For the error bred in the bone. ... Craves what it cannot have, / Not universal love, But to be loved alone." Here was Bork, by his own lights obviously a very great man, and here he had been at the center of the universe for all these years—first as a Yale law professor, then as a judge on the U.S. Court of Appeals for the District of Columbia, lastly as a scholar at The American Enterprise Institute and a revered guest on both *This Week with David Brinkley* and *Larry King Live*—but where was the mighty host of adoring disciples? Never a man to withhold spiritual advice and moral counsel, Bork had been generous with his wisdom, always willing to reward a repentant liberal with one of his golden platitudes. Why then hadn't paradise been regained? Bork had spoken, and yet Clinton was still president; pornographic images still were to be seen in the distant reaches of the Internet, and fourteen-year-old sensualists were still walking around with rings in their noses. Perhaps people weren't listening to Bork, or maybe they had lost their way on the pilgrim road to Washington. But then why had so many of them found Louis Farrakhan, and why were they listening to Howard Stern and begging autographs from Dennis Rodman? The world was an outrage. Let it be scorched and rent asunder, so that the wine mourns, the vine languishes, and the mirth of the lyre is stilled.

The apocalyptic vision is as old as the poetry of Isaiah and as new as the weapons in the hands of the Taliban, the legion of Islamic zealots that conquered most of Afghanistan during the same week in September that the prophet Bork published *Slouching Towards Gomorrah.* I doubt that any of them had a chance to read the book, but even without consulting the judge's chapters on "Intellectuals and Modern Liberalism" or "The Politics of Sex," they seemed to know how to go about the great task of putting an end to the nonsense of liberty and equality. The Taliban insist on a strict construction of the Koran, and within a matter of hours after entering Kabul they established a fairly severe standard of moral conduct—a ban on all music and dancing, the movie theaters closed, women forbidden to work or attend school and allowed to appear in public only if concealed by heavy gowns, men ordered to grow full beards, thieves punished by the cutting off of their hands and feet, children forbidden to fly kites or play marbles, adulterers stoned to death. Maybe not everything that Judge Bork has in mind, but steps in the right direction and certainly an advance on the path of righteousness.

December 1996

La Vie Bohème

> Most artists are sincere and most art is bad, and some
> insincere art (sincerely insincere) can be quite good.
> —Igor Stravinsky

Long ago, before the arrival of the new information order,
when apprentice novelists wrote in longhand and Jack Ker-
ouac was still on the road to Nirvana, I used to associate the
term "avant-garde" with poets in garrets and painters in lofts. I thought
of cheap foreign wine, cold north light, and unreadable manuscripts
bound with string and stored on windowsills next to a photograph of
Ezra Pound and a poster commemorating the glories of fifteenth-century
Florence. None of the associations have survived the last thirty years of
constant revolution within the kingdom of sovereign images, and I now
understand that the genius of the age reveals itself not in the impover-
ishment of its aesthetic sensibility but in the exuberance of its commercial imagination.

Like everybody else in New York who has anything to do with the
media, I probably listen to as many as ten or twelve propositions a
month from people hoping to wrench a profit from one or another of the
new computer technologies—schemes for housing the New York Stock
Exchange on a CD-ROM or reducing Freud's collection of dreams to a
database, designs for search engines that can solve the riddle of the
sphinx, for Web sites that play the music of Beethoven's symphonies or
translate the chronicles of Froissart from the medieval French, twenty-
four-hour commentaries on the Bible, shopping networks that deal in

macadamia nuts and oriental dancing girls.

Most of the technical language I don't understand, but through the mist of talk about info-dynamics and netseek I sometimes can see the heights of the new Parnassus, and I know that instead of perishing from the earth, the means of artistic experiment merely have changed forms—porous systems and agreeable bandwidths in place of an easel or a piano, a spreadsheet instead of four reams of foolscap—and over the course of a single week in late November I listened to three propositions deserving of brief summary, if for no other reason than to measure the distance between Picasso and Polycom. As follows:

A SOURCE FOR ALL SEASONS

Three days after the presidential election, a man wearing a well-cut but nondescript suit showed up in my office to offer his services as the supplier of news for every occasion. He gave his name as "David Cornwall" and looked to be in his early fifties, precise in his choice of words and careful about moving his hands. From a literary agent we both knew he had heard that *Harper's Magazine* sometimes had need of an astonishing rumor or a convenient fact. If so, he could furnish on demand whatever was required.

For twenty years, he said, he had worked at writing novels, but none of his books had sold more than a few thousand copies, and the possibility of a second career occurred to him when he noticed that the better newspaper stories depended upon sources variously identified as "informed," "confidential," "Washington," "high-level," "White House," and "well-placed." Further study persuaded him that the phrases served as a disguise for corporate or government bureaucrats with a grievance.

"Here was a cast of characters easily understood," he said. "People consumed by envy and pitted with malice. All I had to do was assign them an office in the Pentagon or a seat on a campaign plane. I didn't even have to give them names."

First he made himself familiar with the statistical jargon and the standard repertoire of simple political issues. For six months he read government budgets, annual reports, congressional testimony, speeches delivered by corporate presidents at conventions and sales meetings. Once Cornwall had learned what the arguments were likely to be about, he began to work on the problems of motive. Within a year he had developed a plausible technique, making telephone calls to syndicated columnists from an unspecified crossroads within the interior of an obscure bureaucracy. "The Department of Agriculture," he said, "is like Namibia. People think they're supposed to know where it is and what it means, and nobody wants to admit that he never heard of the place."

Emboldened by the credulity of his respondents, Cornwall extended his operations into the lesser provinces of the Departments of Justice and State, appropriating the personae of increasingly prominent government spokesmen and circulating remarks about the murder of Vincent Foster and forthcoming treachery in Islamabad. Pretty soon he began to see his work in print, dressed up in the rubrics of authority, disturbing the peace of nations.

President Clinton's first term in office had proved especially good for business. The congressional committees investigating the Whitewater scandal welcomed any slander of either the President or his wife, and the right-wing newspapers gratefully listened to him speak through the masks of Arkansas state troopers and once-upon-a-time securities brokers doing time for fraud. His collected works he had bound in leather volumes, which he arranged on the desk as if he were a successful author presenting a copy of his new book to Jay Leno or Oprah Winfrey. One of the bound volumes was given over in its entirety to reprints from the *New York Post,* another to reprints from the *Wall Street Journal.*

"You see," he said, not without pride, "what can be done."

Reminding me that *Primary Colors* sold far more copies before its anonymous author was discovered to be Joe Klein, Cornwall stressed the simplicity and low cost of operation. Not only would an editor have more control over the news but the price of the service was a good deal less than the salaries paid to a reporting staff.

Although I could appreciate the financial advantages of the business, I was still at a loss to know what satisfaction Cornwall derived from writing so many similar variations on an identical theme. "An audience," he said. "I'm writing the great American novel, and they read me in Kansas City and Detroit." He left a business card with a single telephone number and seventeen names, most of them listed in CNN's database and all of them protected by the First Amendment.

THE CELEBRITY IPO

At least twenty years younger than Cornwall and dressed in the California manner (blue jeans, silk shirt, ascetic beard, Armani jacket), Meyer was passing briefly through New York on his way to an Oasis concert in London. He was selling ownership in specific individuals whom he had incorporated as public stock offerings—primarily actors and actresses but also a limited number of athletes, musicians, authors, fashion models, and television talk-show hosts. "What we are doing here," he said, "is trading in the currency of images."

Pressed for time, Meyer handed me a sheaf of advertisements for the financial press, together with copies of documents that he had filed with the SEC. The advertisements looked like the ones placed by Merrill Lynch or Morgan Stanley for CDT Systems, or Solectron, or Infonautics—small squares of print listing a name, a date, the sum of the capitalization, and the number of common shares. The filings provided information about the new company's prospective assets and potential liabilities—e.g., teeth, hair, film credits, critical notices, high school batting average, as well as sexual eccentricities, drug habits, and record of prior arrests. Only a few of the names were well known. For the most part they belonged to individuals under the age of twenty.

He explained that nobody these days could become a star without first becoming a celebrity, which was fortunate because celebrity was easier to manufacture than talent or intelligence. The research and development costs were relatively cheap, no more than $15 or $20 million for cosmetic surgery, a biography of some sort, clothes, entertainment, photo opportunities, fees paid to publicists and precinct desk sergeants. As a careful student of the market, especially of the speeds at which images traveled (not only between continents but also between different forms of media), Meyer had worked out a set of equations describing the time it took to transform a guitarist into a T-shirt or a basketball player into a sneaker.

"That's the point, of course," he said. "To change a subject into an object, which, as you well know, is the definition of an American success."

For the cautious investor Meyer provided funds hedged against unforeseen turns in the market: three or four male action heroes balanced with an equal number of female comics, authors of romantic fantasy in the same portfolio with authors of hard-edged detective stories. The adventurous investor could choose more speculative issues, among them a twelve-year-old pitcher in Caracas who could throw a baseball 300 feet and a psychopathic florist recently arrested in Galveston, Texas, on charges of murdering six people in a laundromat after presenting each of them with a yellow rose and a red carnation. The florist hadn't yet been invited to appear on *Good Morning America,* but there was talk of both a book and a movie deal, and Meyer had heard that *The New Yorker* was sending a staff correspondent. It was this last rumor that troubled him. He didn't know if *The New Yorker*'s interest meant that the florist was on the way in or on the way out.

Scornful of the Manhattan media's understanding of show business, he wasn't sure which newspapers and magazines were as accurate as *Variety.* In Los Angeles he had heard it said that once *The New Yorker* decided somebody was important enough to notice, the somebody so favored was already yesterday's news—a dead moon, an old postcard. Did the same rule hold true of *Vanity Fair?* Of *George?* What editors could be trusted to know the difference between a rising and a falling star?

FOND FAREWELLS

In the early 1980s I had known Laughlin as a sculptor briefly famous for decorating the courtyards of suburban office buildings with assemblies of large and ambiguous stone. When the corporations lost their nerve for modernism (at about the same time that the auction and real estate markets collapsed), Laughlin reconstituted himself as a designer of Christmas catalogues. We lost touch, but from mutual friends I heard that he had made a success of the business and that he had been one of the first people to see the possibilities in the television shopping networks, and so I wasn't surprised when he showed up in a state of high good humor, exuding the enthusiasm of a triumphant salesman, the color of his shirt matched to the color of both his shoes and his watch. We exchanged the customary pleasantries about the weather (cold), the effects of the communications revolution (marvelous to behold), and the direction of the twenty-first century (largely in the hands of the Chinese), and then, after the customary moment of expectant silence, Laughlin handed me a catalogue similar to the ones advertising Caribbean resort hotels.

"Designer death," he said. "Like designer flowers or designer chocolate, but better. Much better. More personal."

Looking through the catalogue, I saw that it listed fifty or sixty available deaths in historical order, the "Socrates" followed by the "Julius Caesar," followed by the "Joan of Arc," the "Marie Antoinette," the

"Nelson Rockefeller," the "Robert Maxwell," and the "Kurt Cobain." Accompanied by small but tasteful illustrations, each block of text hinted at the sorts of people likely to be attracted to a particular end. The brochure suggested the "Socrates" for "serene and philosophical individuals no longer besieged by the vanity of human wishes"; the "Nelson Rockefeller" was recommended for the "flamboyant and extroverted personality who delights in astonishing his friends and loved ones."

While I turned the pages, admiring the expensive weight of the paper and the elegance of the typefaces, Laughlin elaborated the marketing strategy in an excited rush of phrases and half-sentences.

"I'm talking spectacles," he said, "for people who have everything but still feel like nobodies. People too rich and too important to die anonymous deaths in sterile hospital rooms. Why shouldn't they go first class—with their names in lights and a chorus of savage tears?"

When I asked him if he expected any trouble with the authorities, if not with the police then with the Christian Coalition or the American Medical Association, he reminded me that Dr. Jack Kevorkian had assisted at forty-six suicides and been acquitted by no fewer than three juries in Michigan. Dismissing my objection as one of no consequence, he continued the sales pitch with unimpaired fervor.

"Like everything else," he said, "it's a question of cost. Take the 'Joan of Arc.' It could be staged anywhere—in Central Park, on the steps of St. Patrick's Cathedral, in a vacant lot; with a cast of jeering thousands, or in front of a few old and quiet friends on a lawn in Connecticut."

He expected different deaths to become fashionable among different sorts of people. He thought that the "Marie Antoinette" or the "Catherine the Great" might appeal to society women; the "Julius Caesar," to literary intellectuals, who tended to hate one another and always could recruit eight or nine of their number willing to stab any author whose book had received a splendid review or stayed on the best-seller list for longer than six weeks.

The brochure wasn't so gauche as to mention prices (available on request), but it was clear that any extra refinements would add substantially to the unit cost. Arrangements could be made for varying intensities of media coverage, for costumes and cameo parts played by well-known actors and political figures, for souvenirs, refreshments, and a farewell message written by an author along the lines of Danielle Steele or John Grisham.

Wondering if I had passed over into the generation no longer comfortable with the experiments of the avant-garde, I asked Laughlin whether some conservative politicians might not think his entertainments insufficiently upbeat.

"Nonsense," he said. "You miss the inspirational angle. Americans are much too afraid of death, and this kind of thing will cure them of their anxiety and hypochondria. Think of the exemplary proofs of human dignity and courage. Think of the relief from boredom."

He could see no flaw in the proposition, but he was having trouble finding investors endowed with entrepreneurial spirit. Thinking that I might know such people, he left me with several copies of the catalogue, and later in the afternoon, reading the small print on the last page, I noticed that a well-designed death also could be a tax deduction. It was possible to make of one's death a charitable entertainment, like a theater performance or a museum benefit. The patron donates his or her death to a worthy cause; everybody enjoys a convivial occasion, the papers publish the guest list, and the proceeds offset the sum of the taxes owed by the deceased's estate.

Reading the final selling point, I couldn't help but admire Laughlin's genius for the new.

January 1997

Economic Correctness

> What I want to see above all is that this remains
> a country where someone can always get rich.
> — RONALD REAGAN

When the Republican majorities in Congress began busying themselves in early December with preliminary investigations of the Lippo Group, the Indonesian cartel said to have supplied extravagant gifts of cash to last year's presidential campaign, the first newspaper reports seemed as straightforward as an old Charlie Chan movie—cunning oriental businessmen lure rich but foolish American tourist into a crooked mah-jongg game in a waterfront opium den. The papers didn't lack for details—President Clinton's exchange of notes and visits with Mochtar Riady, the mysterious comings and goings of John Huang, "disproportionate influence" brought to bear on the making of American foreign policy, large campaign contributions abruptly returned by the Democratic National Committee—and for a few days it looked as if the story was likely to bloom into big news.

But the moral lesson apparently was harder to draw than the headlines implied, and before the month was out I was receiving telephone calls from nervous Washington correspondents in search of experts whom they could consult on the finer points of foreign trade. Did I know anybody reliable on Wall Street, and what was the name of Disney's man who understood the market in offshore bribes? If Air France could hire Senator Dole to sell weekend flights to Paris, what prevented the Lippo Group from hiring President Clinton to sell Coca-Cola in Vietnam? If the global economy was nothing other than a gigantic shopping mall and if an Indonesian billionaire wished to buy an American president instead of an American airplane or an American truck, why make the transaction unpleasant or unnecessarily difficult?

The confusion was both technical and philosophical, and the range of questions suggested that the senior officers of the national news media lacked a doctrine of economic correctness. They knew that under the rules of the new economic world order the value of national sovereignty had been much reduced—becoming roughly equivalent to that of the picturesque backgrounds in an important movie or a trendy restaurant—and they understood that the Japanese already owned most of the Hollywood movie studios, that Rupert Murdoch owned the *New York Post* and Fox News, and that Hachette, a French publishing syndicate, had acquired the franchise on John F. Kennedy, Jr., the best of America's political brand names. But if most of what was worth buying in the American auction already had been sold to foreign bidders, on what text could they construct indignant sermons about the purchase of an already discounted President for a price well below that of an Alaskan forest?

Their most pressing questions I referred to a friend who trades international currencies for Salomon Brothers, but then it occurred to me to make note of the words and phrases that lately have come to express the trend of the times. The meanings flutter in the prevailing wind of opinion like telltales fixed to the mast of a sailboat, and over the course of the last two or three years the definitions appear to have shifted quite a few compass points to the right. The device of an alphabetical list I borrowed from Gustave Flaubert, who compiled his *Dictionary of Accepted Ideas* during the latter half of the nineteenth century and who was thoughtful enough to indicate preferred tones of voice as well as to supply suggestions for apt quotation and supplemental phrase.

ACCOUNTANTS
The unacknowledged legislators of the world.

ARISTOTLE
The first capitalist. He defined slaves as "animated tools" and classified them among the animals and plants.

AWE
Proper show of respect when addressing persons blessed with annual incomes in excess of $52 million. (See FREEDOM.)

BUREAUCRATS

Not to be scoffed at. They're the people who write the tax exemptions. "What else is a banker or a businessman if not an enlightened bureaucrat?"

CAMPAIGN SLOGANS

Political financial products; the equivalents of junk bonds.

CEOS

Heroes of our time. Their decisive habit of mind allows them to order the dismissal of 40,000 superfluous workers without a moment's thought or delay. Refer to them as champions of the people.

CHARITY

The road to hell.

CONSERVATIVE

Ask grandly, "When was America anything other than a conservative country?"

CORPORATION, TRANSNATIONAL

Dominant institution of the late twentieth century, comparable to the medieval Church or the Roman legions in the first century A.D. Because it exists in the realm of pure abstraction (like money and the Holy Ghost), it can give birth to its own parents.

CORRUPTION

Sign of a mature society. The practice of taking bribes teaches the lesson of tolerance.

DEMOCRACY

Outworn system of government, unequal to the tasks of the twenty-first century. A luxury that no first-rate nation can continue to afford. Quote John Adams, "There never was a democracy that did not commit suicide."

ELECTORATE, THE AMERICAN

Suffers from apathy. Compare the affliction to Dutch elm disease, "blighting the forests of freedom."

ETHICS

Local or regional customs, like Basque folk songs or Bolivian hats. Sold at steep discounts in the global economy.

FAMILY VALUES

Sacrosanct. Must be protected at all costs. Avoid attempting to define the phrase.

FASCISM

A much happier and more efficient system of government than generally supposed.

FREEDOM

Synonymous with an income of $52 million a year. (See AWE.)

FREE MARKET

The few people who still question its omniscience are the kind of people who belong to weird religious sects.

FUR COAT

Symbol of democracy. (See MCDONALD'S.)

FUTURE, THE

Under the management of the World Trade Organization in Geneva. The resident clerks envision higher walls, better waste-disposal systems, more prisons.

GENEROSITY

Reckless impulse. Compare it to drunk driving.

GLOBAL ECONOMY

Engineered by wise financiers to guarantee the happiness of mankind. The mechanism is very expensive and very delicate, requiring the participation of investors instead of citizens.

GREED

Tasteless word. Substitute "husbandry" or "prudence."

HAMILTON, ALEXANDER

Recognized at long last as the true father of the country. Praise him without stint. Twenty years ago he was mostly known for having been killed in a duel. His new place in the pantheon of American demigods is founded on his prescience. Well ahead of his time, he understood the importance of banks and child labor. On the latter point, you may quote him directly: "Women and children are rendered more useful, and the latter more early useful, by manufacturing establishments than they would otherwise be."

IDEALISM

Dangerous substance. If left standing too long at room temperature on a library table, idealism congeals into ideology, which breeds totalitarianism and puritanical reigns of virtue. Robespierre was an idealist.

So was Lenin.

INDIVIDUALISM

Priceless commodity.

LIBERAL

Synonym for anything weak, soft, effeminate, obsolete, or un-American. Always pronounced with an intonation of scorn. Four years ago the rules of rhetorical decency obliged President Bush to mask the insult with a euphemism—"the L word." The Dole campaign could afford to speak more plainly. The country in the meantime had learned to properly evaluate the ruinous cost of good intentions.

LITERATURE

Decorative art; belongs to the same category of ornament as throw pillows and lawn sculpture.

MCDONALD'S

Symbol of democracy. (See FUR COAT.)

MONEY

The light of the world and the mandate of Heaven. Impossible to say enough in its favor.

MONOPOLY

Glorious manifestation of human ingenuity. The source of all our blessings. Why the department stores never run out of Italian suits and French cologne.

MULTICULTURALISM

The department stores understand it better than the universities.

NATIONALISM

Last refuge of small and impoverished countries without a well-developed tourist trade. Instead of tennis courts and boat marinas they have street riots and torn flags.

OUTRAGE

In short supply. Driven off the market during the last two years by the 70 percent rise of the Dow Jones Industrial Average. When Dole asked after its whereabouts during the final, desperate week of last November's presidential campaign, he was informed by the polls that it was where it was supposed to be—stored safely in the attic with the Bob Dylan records.

POLITICS

Expensive pastime, like golf or hang gliding. Once enjoyed by farmers and populists; now pursued mostly by people who can afford their own airplanes.

POOR, THE

By-products of the global economy. They perform a necessary service, reminding people more fortunately placed that the advancement of learning does not come cheap, that civilization entails sacrifice.

In the early months of the Clinton Administration it was thought that the government might do something on behalf of the poor. But that was before the poor were redefined as object lessons and cautionary tales. To make them rich would destroy their purpose.

PROFITS

Never indecent or obscene.

RUSSIANS

They brought ruin on themselves because for seventy-four years they forgot that money is God.

SELF-INTEREST

Always preceded by "enlightened." Worthy cause. The Puritan forefathers believed that God's grace revealed itself as property.

SMITH, ADAM

Great man. Praise him without stint. The eighteenth-century avatar of Bill Gates.

SUPERFLUOUS

Word applied to people, never to hotels or automobiles.

TECHNOLOGY

Indispensable. Hard to remember how one got along without it.

UNEMPLOYMENT

Necessary check on inflation.

UTOPIA

Once imagined as a place, or at least as a possible destination. Now understood as a state of mind and an escape from stress, as near at hand as a prescription for Prozac or the next plane to Florida.

VIRTUE

Best practiced by the poor, who have more need of it.

WARS

The only important ones involve large corporations, not nation-states.

ZAIRE

Corrupt country in Africa. Proves the futility of giving money to people who don't understand it. Once famous for elephants.

February 1997

The Spanish Armadillo

The map appears to us more real than the land.

—D. H. LAWRENCE

W hen I agreed late last summer to go to New Orleans in early January for the celebration of what would have been the late Bernard DeVoto's one hundredth birthday, I made the mistake of thinking that I could meet the rhetorical demands of the occasion with a few words of well-turned praise. What I knew of DeVoto, I knew from reading his more famous books—*1846: The Year of Decision, Across the Wide Missouri, The Course of Empire, Mark Twain's America.* I knew him as a first-rate historian, passionate in his feeling for the nineteenth-century American West, and as a fine writer whose accounts of the long line of ox-drawn wagons lumbering across the plains from the Missouri River to Fort Laramie and South Pass had shaped much of my own imagining of the Oregon Trail.

But the program called for me to speak about DeVoto in his character as a journalist, specifically as the author of the monthly column appearing in *Harper's Magazine* (from 1935 until his death in 1955) under the rubric "The Easy Chair," and these writings I knew only by hearsay. From time to time at a New York literary assembly I would run across a senior member of the city's publishing faculty, who would say that if I took the trouble to read DeVoto in "The Easy Chair" I might learn something useful about American politics and the English language.

Born in Odgen, Utah, under the western slope of the Wasatch Mountains, the son of a Mormon father and a Catholic mother (both apostate),

157

DeVoto attended public high school and Harvard University before settling, in 1927, in Cambridge, Massachusetts. His presence in the East strengthened his fierce affection for the West, and his writing is everywhere marked by poignant remembrance of western landscapes, western grasses, western animals and birds.

From his photographs and from people who knew him well, I gathered that he was somewhat similar in appearance to H. L. Mencken, a heavy smoker (cigarettes, not cigars) who didn't mince his words and wore his convictions on his sleeve. By nature contrarian, he undertook the writing of "The Easy Chair" in the spirit of dissent and as a matter of civic obligation. The American democracy he understood as an idea in motion and a set of principles constantly in need of further experiment and revision. Against the impulse to declare the experiment complete (an impulse easily confused by the wellborn and comfortably placed with the will of Divine Providence), DeVoto construed "The Easy Chair" as a relentless questioning of whatever temporary wisdom chanced to have been elected to political or literary office.

What was remarkable was not only DeVoto's broad canvas of topics—the fascist components of McCarthyism, the improper manufacture of kitchen knives and the proper manufacture of a martini, the feckless destruction of the public land and the national forest (by rapacious timber and mining interests that enjoyed, then as now, the blessings of a compliant Congress), the Mexican and Civil wars, detective novels, Marxism, the Union Pacific Railroad, sagebrush, and the FBI—but also his many tones of voice: sardonic, whimsical, poetic, angry, puckish, romantic, mocking, philosophical.

Often at odds with his peers in the literary trades, he detested flag-waving patriots, thought Harry Truman too conservative in his politics and Thomas Wolfe too liberal with his adjectives, never tired of emptying the slops of ridicule on the heads of imbecile novelists and crooked politicians. Many of his columns read as if they had been written last week, and following their progress through the pages of *Harper's Magazine,* I marked enough passages to teach a semester's course in what DeVoto would have called "the technic" of declamatory prose.

ON GOVERNMENT SURVEILLANCE: Announcing in 1949 (i.e., long before it was safe to do so) that henceforth he would refuse to cooperate with government investigations loosed upon the citizenry by the House Un-American Activities Committee or the FBI—"I like a country where it's nobody's damned business what magazines anyone reads, what he thinks, whom he has cocktails with. I like a country where we do not have to stuff the chimney against listening ears. ... We had that kind of country a little while ago, and I'm for getting it back. It was a lot less scared than the one we've got now."

ON BAD WRITING: With specific reference to Miss Gertrude Stein, "whose art had no connection whatever with life or death, love or hate, rejoicing or grief, success or failure, belief or doubt, any other emotion of mankind, any experience of anyone, or any of the values that enable people to live together—an art which floated freely in a medium of pure caprice sustained by nothing except its awareness of its own inner wondrousness."

ON DEMOCRACY: Relieving Walter Lippmann in 1939 of the delicate impression that democratic government is a stately exchange of highminded, nonpartisan views among the senior members of the Century Club, that it somehow can be washed clean of envy, jealousy, or greed, that it is ever anything other than the work of ordinary men, bewildered, groping, at cross-purposes, verbose—"The Senate had not forgotten, as Mr. Lippmann had, that this is a democracy. The Senators are politicians, much less clever than you or I, much more steeped in partisanship than Mr. Lippmann. They are certain to befog its issues with deplorable ignorance, certain to distort them with partisan interests of political parties, personal candidacies, business interests and pressure groups.... Thank God!"

ON RADICAL CHIC: Speaking in 1940 of a doe-eyed leftist intellectual who had supported the "brave and wholly literary rebellion" of Marxism with the enthusiasm of an inherited fortune and abruptly found himself betrayed by Stalin's pact with Hitler—"You can say something, if uselessly, to a friend whose child has died, whose wife has left him, whose ambition has been wrecked. But what can you say to a friend whose god has died?"

No matter what the topic at hand, DeVoto's strength as a writer springs from his understanding that history is a continuous narrative, as closely bound to time future as to time past. His Mormon grandfather climbed the grade of the Platte River in company with Brigham Young, and, once arrived in the Utah Valley under the auspices of the angel Moroni, he resurrected the dead land with apple orchards, and where he found the earth poisoned with volcanic ash he made it sweet with cottonwood trees.

Two of DeVoto's most somber columns draw the lines of historical perspective on the blackboard of the Second World War. The German armies invaded Poland on September 1, 1939, but the printing schedule of *Harper's Magazine* delayed DeVoto's response until the November issue and a column entitled "The Oncoming." He begins with his listening to the news of the invasion on a car radio in the hills of northern Vermont. The far-off voices, urgent and broken by static, remind him of a bright afternoon in August 1914, in the Rocky Mountains. The German armies have marched into Belgium, and DeVoto is seventeen years old, at work in a newspaper office, copying the bulletins from the Associated Press wire onto long strips of cheap paper and hanging the news in the windows from lengths of twine. The pictures in his head are those of a storybook war—Uhlans sitting astride their horses against the Belgian sky at twilight, British destroyers putting hurriedly to sea, columns of dust-gray troops marching through fields of ripening wheat—all pretty pictures, as romantic as Sir Lancelot and as far away as Saturn. The nostalgic sentiment doesn't last as long as the next sentence. Correcting it at once with the counterweight of history (the sum of the dead at Château-Thierry and Verdun, what happened to President Wilson's useless Fourteen Points) and knowing that "this time the war will be neither distant nor romantic, even to boys," DeVoto wonders what will become of America and what he will say to his nine-year-old son. He measures the likely cost of the war by the loss of individual liberty, even among the victors, and by the probable transformation of "a nation that never quite existed" into something a good deal closer in character and tone to an authoritarian bureaucracy.

The questions lead DeVoto first to the thought that his son will not grow up in the America in which he was born, and then, bearing in mind his grandfather's trees, to the further thought, "but neither did I, or anyone else who has ever lived here." America is about making the best of what can be made of circumstances usually adverse, and the cost of any life is the price asked for it, which, as often as not, comes down to a "belief in a right and truth that do not exist, conscription in a war against the uncomprehended for reasons never given."

A similarly hard-edged realism informs a column that DeVoto introduces five years later with the sentences, "You may remember the Lost Generation. It was primarily a literary phenomenon, an invention of novelists." By April 1944 the end of the Second World War was plainly in sight, and DeVoto sets out to forestall a reprise of the self-pity that became fashionable in the 1920s. The trope of the Lost Generation he attributes to Ernest Hemingway and finds "sickly and unclean," a cliché much in vogue among college boys drinking iced gin under potted palms, noding their glossy heads and tapping their glossy shoes in time to a Cole Porter tune, saying that their finer feelings had been so bruised by the ugliness of war that "they saw quite through life's hollow shams." DeVoto very much hopes that this time there will be none of that. Yes, the conditions of life are not what any of us would choose—"It is too bad that we grow old, too bad that we prove less admirable than we thought, too bad that love fails, ambition peters out, friends die, dreams come to nothing"—but the waste and failure of an individual does not mean that "God had it in for him" or that "a private pain in the bowels" proves the theorem of the world's evil.

Again it is DeVoto's sense of history (of the generations belonging to the same repertory company, succeeding one another on the same stage) that enlarges his argument. He is not talking merely about literary affectation. Simultaneously and in the same wide lens with the languid tableau of the Lost Generation posed in tuxedos and evening gowns against a Manhattan skyline, DeVoto sees the wounded armies of the Potomac and Northern Virginia, walking home from the Civil War without shoes, wearing ragged and stinking clothes, carrying with them the memories of panic, hunger, lice, dysentery, and their friends blown to bloody shreds, and, whether they were going South or North, "the best years of their youth devoured by war, no fine thing done, no fine thing possible in the time remaining."

And what became of that generation, and who among them sang the sad songs of self-pity? Instead of admiring the symbolic impotence of Jake Barnes, they went out and sold the crops, repaired the farm, "broke the prairies, dug the mines, occupied the West, built the railroads, manned the industry that remade the world."

The celebration of DeVoto's centennial birthday took place on January 11, at Le Petite Théâtre in the New Orleans French Quarter, across St. Peter Street from the old Spanish building in which, on December 20, 1803, the envoys of Napoleon transferred to the agents of Thomas Jefferson the deed to the Louisiana Purchase. An audience of maybe two hundred people, almost all of them over the age of fifty, listened to a series of appreciative remarks by DeVoto's son, Mark, by Stephen Ambrose, Patricia Limerick, and Arthur Schlesinger, Jr. The program occupied the whole of the day, and as I listened to the several scholars talk about different aspects of DeVoto's work (his editing of the Lewis and Clark journals, his efforts on behalf of the public lands), it was easy enough to think of the objections that could be raised against his telling of the American tale—overly triumphant, too many white men in the foreground and not enough women in the scene, too idealistic a faith in Manifest Destiny.

Some of the objections no doubt could be sustained, but what struck me even more forcibly were the differences between DeVoto's language—rooted in fact and grounded in narrative—and our own postliterate drift of images set to the music of television. Narrative becomes a picturesque montage (like a commercial for Calvin Klein's Obsession or movies as flaccid as *The English Patient*), and the distinctions between time present and time past dissolve into the mirrors of the eternal present. The effects are sometimes marvelous to behold, but how do we write history in a language like Gertrude Stein's, one that floats freely "in a medium of pure caprice sustained by nothing except its awareness of its own inner wondrousness," and if we don't know how to tell our own story, then how do we know who we are?

DeVoto enjoyed the luxury of writing for people who still knew how to read (and who placed as high a value on the stores of public memory as they did on the Colorado River or any other natural resource), but he died before the advent of twenty-four-hour television and never had to ask himself how it might be possible to join the art of literary narrative with the acts of the historical imagination in the floating worlds of timeless fantasy.

With respect to the number of illiterate citizens at large in the United States at present, the official estimate of 40 million seems optimistically low. The statistics published by the Department of Education measure the capacity to read road signs and restaurant menus. Complicate the proceedings by one or two degrees of further comprehension (an acquaintance with a minimal number of standard texts, the capacity to recognize the tone of irony), and the number of people impaired by a lack of literary intelligence probably comes nearer to 200 million. The evidence for the higher estimate shows up in proofs as various as the simplification of the vocabulary adjusted to the demands of television news broadcasts (simple verbs, no compound sentences, nouns in one or two syllables, no dependent clauses), the clubfooted prose that disfigures many of the books on the Sunday best-seller lists, the poorly written examination papers pronounced summa cum laude at the country's leading universities.

Three years ago at Yale I taught a course of English composition and found only four of twelve students in the class capable of writing a well-arranged paragraph—not because they weren't intelligent but because they never had acquired the habit of reading. Familiar with a vast archive of visual images, they easily could recall scenes and fragments of scenes from *Star Wars, Melrose Place, Late Night with David Letterman, Pulp Fiction, Masterpiece Theatre,* and *Twin Peaks,* but books were grim tasks instead of pleasant diversions: foreign objects, unfamiliar and vaguely ominous, meant to be studied as if they were cancer cells multiplying under the lens of a microscope or a jigsaw puzzle constructed from the bones of triceratops.

Similar observations have been made by a great many other people remarking on the progress of American education over the last thirty years, but never more entertainingly than by Richard Lederer in 1987 in the *Maine Sunday Telegram.* A teacher at the Saint Paul's School in Concord, New Hampshire, Lederer had pieced together a history of the world from sentences then appearing in classrooms (eighth grade to first year of college) across the whole of the United States:

"The inhabitants of ancient Egypt were Mummies. They ... traveled by Camelot."
"The Greeks invented three kinds of columns—Corinthian, Doric, and Ironic. They also had myths. A myth is a female moth."
"The government of England was a limited mockery."
"Sir Francis Drake circumcised the world with a 100-foot clipper."
"When Elizabeth exposed herself before her troops, they all shouted, 'Hurrah.' Then her navy went out and defeated the Spanish armadillo."

The transference of the nation's preferred forms of expression from the idioms of print to those of the electronic media bears out the projection set forth as long ago as 1964 by Marshall McLuhan in *Understanding*

Media. McLuhan began with the premise that content follows form ("We become what we behold"; "We shape our tools, and thereafter our tools shape us") and so proceeded to an analogy between the nineteenth-century invention of the electric lightbulb and the fifteenth-century invention of movable type. Just as the printing press made possible the overthrow of a settled aesthetic and political order, so also did the practical applications of electricity—as telephone, telegraph, computer, CD-ROM, fiber optics, etc.—give rise to new structures of feeling and thought. The full force of the second epistemological revolution has yet to be fully grasped or acknowledged, but to complain about the events in progress is to stand firmly on the side of the medieval thrones and dominions who railed against Gutenberg's typefaces as the heralds of intellectual anarchy and "the end of civilization as we know it." It's easy enough to deplore the differences between Cicero and Howard Stern, but the more interesting questions have to do with what happens next. Is it possible to make an adult language from an alphabet of brightly illustrated children's blocks?

The sensibility shaped by the electronic media over the last forty-odd years has by now acquired a distinctive form: impatient, easily bored, geared to increasingly short bursts of attention, intuitive, musical, tuned to abrupt changes of mood and scene. Most importantly, it is a sensibility bereft of memory. The past is constantly dissolving into the eternal present, and the time is always now, if not on Channel 4 in New York or Los Angeles, then on Channels 27 and 41 in London or Rangoon. Memory is a subject for librarians, but even the best of them cannot keep pace with the accelerated compression of time into smaller and smaller fragments. Look at a movie made thirty years ago and the epic storm at sea lasts for half an hour; now it comes and goes in four minutes. Television commercials that in the 1960s needed two minutes to tell their story have been reduced to fifteen seconds. News documentaries resolve into a sequence of flash cards, and music videos shift back and forth at two-second intervals between as many as four lines of contrapuntal sexual fantasy.

Narrative becomes montage, and the rules of grammar and syntax give way to the arranging of symbolic icons in mosaics like those made from the flashing signs in Times Square. Nothing necessarily follows from anything else. If it so happens that President Clinton's State of the Union Address occupies the same moment in time as the award of the verdict in the O.J. Simpson civil trial, the camera embraces both events without transition or the presumption of cause and effect. The images of power and celebrity signify nothing other than their own transitory glory, and like the moon acting upon the movement of the tides, the divinities of Planet Hollywood (Madonna, Michael Jordan, next week's serial killer, the President of the United States) call forth the collective surges of emotion that rise and fall with as little apparent meaning as the surf breaking on the beach at Santa Monica. Knowledge becomes a matter of instantly recognizing patterns rather than an act of sequential thought. One understands that the United States Senate is not a golf ball, that Liz Claiborne is a dress, and that it wasn't Bill Cosby who killed Nicole Brown Simpson, and the making of these connections (as many as 12,000 of them in the course of an afternoon's shopping and an evening's programming) constitutes the proof of genius and the sum of wisdom.

Closer in character to poetry than prose, the electronic media proceed by analogy and synecdoche—the face of a hungry Rwandan child standing as surrogate for the continent of Africa, a helicopter shot of an Iowa village green expressing the boundless store of American virtue. The constant viewer learns to accept the images on the screen as metaphors, all of them weightless and without consequence, all of them returning as surely as the sun—reworked and rearranged as other commercials, other press conferences, other football seasons—demanding nothing of the audience except the duty of ritual observance.

Maybe the technology is still too new. Twenty years haven't passed since the general introduction of the personal computer; the World Wide Web has been in place for no more than eight years; even the television networks, despite their mechanical sophistication and longer term of experiment, haven't yet evolved past the stage of complicated toys. Add all the instruments of the electronic media into the orchestra of their high-speed parts, and they can do little more than speak to themselves in rebuses—short words intercut with pictures like those in a third-grade geography book. The language is made for billboards and better suited to selling a product than to expressing a thought. The forms invite development of their implicit poetics—toward the density of the Japanese haiku and the pointillism of Georges Seurat, in the direction of computer games on the order of Myst or Civilization—but in the excited rush into cyberspace (wiring every circuit to every other circuit, staking claims to anything and everything that can be outfitted as an icon or shipped by satellite to Shanghai) few people have taken the trouble to explore the possibilities. The television and movie cameras still drift through too many pointless silences and too much dead air, the voice-overs serving as captions instead of polyphonic counterpoint, and much of the writing on the Internet could as easily be posted in spray paint on the side of a bus.

Much of the current dissatisfaction with the electronic media suggests that their prospective audiences are a good deal more perceptive than they are dreamed of in the marketing theory of Time Warner and Fox Television (cf. the diminished network ratings, the improved standing of C-SPAN, the ability of twelve-year-olds to simultaneously listen to Beck, watch *Friends,* and work problems in advanced algebra), and before too long I expect the editors at *Wired* to discover Hermann Hesse's novel *The Glass Bead Game.*

Hesse didn't use the term "virtual reality," but he was confronted with the overthrow of a settled aesthetic and political order in the Germany of the 1930s, as well as with the advent of the electronic cultural dispensation in the person of Adolf Hitler. Plotting an escape into a realm of pure symbol and disembodied mind, he imagined a language of abstract signs representative of all the noble thoughts and works of art conceived by the mind of man on the long journey through recorded time. Analogous to the Egyptian hieroglyph and the Chinese ideogram, the vocabulary of the Glass Bead Game presents its adepts with an instrument on which, as if on a vast organ of "almost unimaginable perfection," they might play the music of the spheres and render the whole of the intellectual cosmos in forms equivalent to the toccata, passacaglia, prelude, and fugue. A single glass bead stands for a motif as specific as the diagram of a plant cell, a sentence from Leibniz or the Upanishads, a conjunction of planets in the year 1348, a line from Shakespeare's *Coriolanus,* a cross-section of the human heart, or the first four bars of Beethoven's Fourth Piano Concerto. The players of the game belong to a monastic order in the forests of Castalia (a spiritual province set apart from the kingdoms of politics and economics), and once a year they come together under the direction of the master of the game (the Magister Ludi) to compose, on what Hesse imagines as a musical staff as large as a cathedral wall, the "unio mystica." The audience consists of intellectuals of all ranks, physicists as well as architects and philologists, sufficiently familiar with the symbolism to appreciate the intention of the metaphysical themes and variations.

Hesse's bead game lends itself so obviously to the transcendental aspirations of the Internet that it's probably only a matter of months before Microsoft buys the rights to his name for one of its software programs. Maybe in the fullness of compressed time we will evolve a language made from the glyphs and signs of the more familiar popular culture, with the Nike swoosh and Ralph Lauren's polo player, the logos for Coca-Cola, Mercedes-Benz, and the National Football League, with photographs of the white Ford Bronco, Warhol's soup cans, and Marilyn Monroe.

My own introduction to the set of circumstances recognized by Hesse and codified by McLuhan took place in the early 1970s when I was asked by NBC television to consider writing a documentary about what was then known as "the energy crisis." The network had gone to no small trouble or expense to collect nineteen hours of handsome film footage of Arab oil sheiks and American politicians, of tankers riding at anchor in New York Harbor or streaming through the Strait of Hormuz, long lines of cars at California gas stations—but nobody knew what the pictures were supposed to mean. Until the producers decided what it was they wanted to say—bad Arabs, good Americans; good Arabs, bad Americans; oil reserves plentiful and cheap; oil reserves expensive and scarce—they might as well have been staring at nineteen hours of empty sky. Because none of the people in the room knew anything about the oil business other than what they had read on the front page of the *New York Times,* I could foresee a long series of meetings likely to lead nowhere except back to the front page of the *New York Times,* and I wondered why the network didn't borrow the practice of David Hockney—cut the paper into little pieces, paste up the words on a studio wall, and film the collage from six angles over the top of Edwin Newman's head.

Although I declined the NBC proposition, some years later I accepted an offer from a British production company to write a six-hour television documentary about America's wars in the twentieth century, and in the course of doing so I discovered what McLuhan meant by the phrase "The medium is the message." Allotted forty-three seconds and seventy-eight words in which to explain the origins of the Second World War, while at the same time providing a transition from still photographs of Neville Chamberlain at the Munich Peace Conference in 1938 to newsreel footage of the German Luftwaffe bombing Poland in September 1939, I understood that television bears more of a resemblance to symbolist poetry than it does even to newspaper prose. The camera looks but doesn't see, and the necessary compression forces both the words and the images to become less literal and more figurative.

Twenty-three years after the late President Richard M. Nixon was frog-marched out of the White House, the single word "Watergate" brings to mind not only the burglaries at the building of that name but also a film montage intercutting scenes of the Vietnam War with the face of Sam Irvin superimposed on the faces of H. R. Haldeman and Archibald Cox, Henry Kissinger's voice mixed with the sound of incoming artillery at Danang, clouds of tear gas drifting across college lawns and the steps of the Pentagon, Nixon himself waving goodbye from the door of the helicopter on the White House lawn.

The Watergate metaphor replaced the Camelot metaphor (another trope made to the specifications of the electronic media), and by the winter of 1975 what was once a land of orchards and sweet-running streams had become a desert inhabited by foul and crawling things. Before Watergate, most politicians were presumed trustworthy until proven guilty of fraud or discovered with a Mafia kingpin in a Baltimore hotel. Maybe not all of them were as handsome as Jack Kennedy or as earnest as Jimmy Stewart in *Mr. Smith Goes to Washington,* but it was thought that they were not the kind of people who accepted money from Chinese arms merchants or licked a prostitute's toes.

The towers of Camelot and the ruin of Watergate serve as the two sovereign metaphors for the political history of the United States over the last quarter of a century. Each president subsequent to Kennedy and Nixon has attempted to ally his administration with the glory of the former (behold, another knight come to the Round Table) and sentence his opponent (treacherous friend to the traitor Mordred) to the dungeons of the latter. Every scandal worthy of the name aspires to the ignominy of the suffix "gate" (Irangate, Troopergate, etc.), and on the sunnier side of the proposition, the writers of political ad copy strive for phrases that will restore to government the charm of musical comedy—"Morning in America," "A thousand points of light," "A place called Hope."

Although the tropes seldom accomplish all they intend, they conform to the rules of Hesse's *Das Glasperlenspiel* and meet the requirements of the electronic media. Instead of narrative we have montage, and our perceptions being tuned to the surfaces of film rather than to the structures of print, we tell one another stories not by lining up rows of words but by making connections (sometimes synchronous, sometimes in juxtaposition) between the film loops stored in our heads. Words define themselves not as signs of a specific meaning but as symbols bearing lesser or greater weights of cinematic association, and history becomes a form of film criticism.

Although not yet as densely imprinted as the word "Watergate," the runes "O. J.," "Disney," "Lincoln bedroom," "Microsoft," "Greenspan," and "Bork" all evoke a series of images from which I could construct—as if from a strand of DNA—the whole of America's recent social, political, and economic history. Aligned with images of both Rodney and Martin Luther King (one of them prostrate on a Los Angeles freeway, the other standing before a crowd on the Washington Mall), O. J. signifies black; set in the context of the NFL (another not inconsiderable trope), O. J. connotes talent; matched with Heidi Fleiss, O. J. conjugates as decadence, Hollywood celebrity, or the vagaries of California jurisprudence. "Microsoft" and "Lincoln bedroom" lend themselves to similar sets of changes, similar to those improvised by a jazz musician taking liberties with a standard melody, or Hesse's Magister Ludi setting up beads in the Academy at Castalia.

No wonder the historian finds it hard to tell a straight story. The prospective readers think in circles. Conversant with the wandering paths through cyberspace (click on genetics, go to Pleistocene) and accustomed to the dissolving images seen on the eleven o'clock news or in the movies of Oliver Stone, the audience imprisoned within the walls of the electronic media inhabits the illusion of a once-upon-a-time in which Eva Perón is a model for Yves St. Laurent and a friend of Andrew Lloyd Webber, and Jane Austen is forever riding in a carriage on the road to Bath.

How then to salvage from the past any meaning that doesn't instantly collapse into surrealist fantasy, a collage by David Hockney, or, together with *The English Patient*, an epic television commercial for a perfume yet to be named? By the historians whom I've read in the last several years, the question seems to me best answered by Evan Connell in *Son of the Morning Star*. The book takes up the subject of what is now known as the Battle of the Little Bighorn, where, on June 25, 1876, General George A. Custer led five companies of the 7th Cavalry into an armed mob of yipping and barking Unkpapa Sioux, who promptly made his name a synonym for glory. But instead of trying to reconstruct a patriotic melodrama, Connell deconstructs one of the more elaborate metaphors in the syllabus of American myth. He proceeds by digression and conducts an interrogation of the surviving facts. Curious about all facets of that unfortunate afternoon and careful to distinguish between what is known and what can be surmised, Connell inquires about everything—Custer's horse, Dandy, the prior service records of Major Reno and Captain Benteen, Sioux burial scaffolds, steamboat navigation on the Yellowstone River, the practice of taking scalps, the rate of fire expected of a .44 caliber Remington revolver, buffalo skulls, Crazy Horse preparing himself for battle by painting white hailstones on his body and tying a brown pebble behind one ear. As the details accumulate, they extend and compound one another, and the reader who stays the course of Connell's curiosity comes away with the sense of a weightless flag having been grounded on the field of human experience and clearly marked on the map of time.

Were I to teach history either to grammar-school or college students, I would borrow from the example of Connell and address a year's course to a cross-section of time as brief as a week but under no circumstances longer than six months. Making a foreground of a single set of events—let's say the Constitutional Convention assembled in Philadelphia in the summer of 1787—I would begin with Benjamin Franklin, a benevolent gentleman of eighty-one known for his gargantuan sexual appetite as well as for his wisdom, seated between Alexander Hamilton and James Madison for the occasion of the convention's opening on June 15, on a little platform raised one short step above the chairs arranged for the other fifty-odd delegates gathered in the statehouse to draw the blueprint of a republic for which, as Madison informed the company, "there had been no precedent in the whole of history." Madison kept careful notes of the proceedings of the next three months, and to the text in hand I would add concentric rings of historical circumstance—first the size and condition of the city of Philadelphia, understood at the time as a sink of iniquity and a capital of dissipation, its sidewalks and gutters paved with brick but reeking with the stench of horse and human excrement, the Quaker drawing rooms crowded with card tables and crystal bowls of rum, pigs rooting through the quagmire of the streets for spoiled vegetables and rotted oysters, fashionable ladies followed on their afternoon walks by black slave boys carrying their toilet cases and bonbon boxes.

The convention took place in secret, behind windows stuffed with felt and no word of the arguments among the uniformly prosperous delegates (forty of them owed money by the Congress and fifteen owning slaves) released to the rabble-rousing press. The gentlemen in fine broadcloth and brocade had come to arrange the political affairs of the new nation in ways convenient to their own economic interests, and by describing the nature of those interests, I could extend the circles of reference into Virginia and Massachusetts, and then, by again widening the lens but still in the summer of 1787, to the Indian frontier in western Pennsylvania and the tennis court at Versailles, or possibly as far as Russia, where Catherine the Great was making her tour of Potemkin's artificial villages (not so different from the ones imagined by Hillary Rodham Clinton on her travels through the American Midwest), or to Prague, where Mozart that year conducted the first performance of *Don Giovanni.*

If at the end of the term the students at least had learned that the parade floats marched across the screen of the news go nowhere except around in circles, I would count the course a success. Because the camera seems to impart meaning where no meaning exists, too often I meet people who think it sufficient merely to recognize the name and shape of Tom Cruise or Newt Gingrich, and that by stringing their symbols like beads on a therapeutic thread of private reverie, they have said something both public and profound. Apparently it never occurs to them that they speak a language of prerecorded experience and ready-made cliché, geared to the specifications of a machine in a magic kingdom where, in Simone Weil's apt but bleak phrase, "It is the thing that thinks, and the man who is reduced to the state of the thing."

March, April, May 1997

Field Trip

Don't get thinking it's a real country because you
can get a lot of high school kids into gym suits and
have them spell out "bananas" for the newsreels.
— F. SCOTT FITZGERALD

*L*ast winter's performance in Washington of the play entitled
"Our American Government" didn't come up to the mini-
mum standards suggested by F. Scott Fitzgerald. The gym
suits kept slipping down around the knees of the Republican cheerlead-
ers on Capitol Hill, and every time the Democrats lined up to spell the
word "bananas" they found that one of the letters had been sold to a
Chinese arms merchant or lost by Webster Hubbell.

Between early January and late March, the stories from Washington
were unanimous in their descriptions of futility, incompetence, and
fraud. At the White House, President Clinton was confined to both a
wheelchair and the pillory of scandal. Every new proof of his greed for
campaign money added to the weight of accusation, which by Valen-
tine's Day had become as disabling as the wooden stocks in which the
old New England Puritans placed the companions of Satan.

The 105th Congress meanwhile had approached a similar state of
inconsequence. The House Ethics Committee in January reprimanded
Newt Gingrich, the Speaker of the House, on grounds that he was either
a crook or a fool, and the Speaker's subsequent loss of stature deprived
the Republican majorities in both the House and the Senate of the
primum mobile meant to drive their legislative agenda. Nearly a hundred

days had come and gone without a decisive vote on any large item of
public business—on the budget, on health care or education, on taxes or
campaign-finance reform. At a loss for anything else to do, the Republicans had passed the time marking up the bills of recrimination, blaming
the Democrats and one another for causing the trouble with the gym
suits.

The New York reviews of the performance were uniformly bad, and
over the course of the winter I encountered a good many people quick to
express either mockery or disdain. As early as the first week in February
a public opinion poll sponsored by Fox News confirmed the popular
feeling of disgust—a clear majority of the respondents agreeing with the
statement that politicians were less apt to tell the truth than prostitutes—and by the end of the month I noticed that I was making the case
for the defense.

Too many people in New York fail to appreciate the purpose of the
federal government, which is to promote the illusion of progress while at
the same time preserving the comfort and convenience of the status quo.
The substance of change brings with it the bitterness of limitation and
restraint; the appearance of change requires only the staging of
words—embracing the platitudes of the moment, postponing the difficult decisions until the next committee meeting or the next election,
defining the passions likely to excite a dormant electorate as disruptions
that must be smoothed over, not as questions that might be answered or
responsibilities that must be met.

The distinctions were never easy to explain, but they became increasingly awkward as Congress and the White House continued to explore
each other's compost heaps in search of soiled money and rotten promises. By early April, I was beginning to feel the need for reassurance, and
so I boarded a train to Washington on the same day that the House of
Representatives returned from its Easter recess.

The day was bright blue, the cherry trees in bloom and the tulips as
red as the blood of patriots. By a stroke of good fortune, I found myself
climbing the stairs on the west front of the Capitol with a troop of
touring Girl Scouts, and as I listened to their guide name the marble
figures of the presidents standing around the perimeter of the Rotunda,
I pitied the poor skeptics in New York obliged to breathe the foul air of
cynicism.

The first of the day's press conferences, a joint announcement of Republican purpose and resolve by the managers of the majorities in the

Senate and the House, took place in the office of the Speaker, and I was glad to see Gingrich in the center of a row of lesser politicians, seated bolt upright behind a plain wooden table, as bright-eyed and cocksure as an alert parrot. Among the more sardonic newspaper people it had been rumored that Gingrich was still hiding in closets, but during the last few weeks he had been traveling in China, and there among the ancient scrolls he apparently had recovered his persona as "a teacher of the rules of civilization," instructing assorted Chinese officials in the meaning of liberty and the consequences of failing to meet their obligations to the cause of human rights and the principle of free trade. On the evening previous to his reappearance in Congress, Gingrich had told a crowd of cheering acolytes at the Ritz Carlton Hotel about the great esteem in which he was held in the Orient, offering as proof a story culled from the *Washington Post* (the treacherous, liberal *Washington Post*) about how it had come to pass in far-off Mongolia that an old herdsman in a canvas yurt (subsisting on "chunks of sheep fat and shots of fermented mare's milk to ward off the unspeakable cold") had chanced upon a text of Gingrich's Contract with America. The revelation roused the herdsman from his primitive torpor, and he went forth to bring democracy to the forsaken steppes once ruled by Genghis Khan. If the word of Gingrich could accomplish so much at so great a distance, think what it could accomplish in the nearby precincts of Pennsylvania Avenue.

Gingrich administered the restorative bombast (balanced budget, destruction of the IRS, etc.) with the verve of a latter-day Polonius or Dr. Pangloss, and although he declined to answer questions about how and when he would pay the $300,000 fine imposed on him by the Ethics Committee, on the matters of state he was happy to say that everything was for the best in this best of all possible worlds. The reporters pressing against the conference table flapped their notebooks and shouted questions, but Gingrich dismissed them with a gesture signifying their irrelevance, and I for one was thankful for the decisiveness of his rebuke. A few of the questions might have proven rude or out of place, like gum wrappers dropped on the floor of the Rotunda.

The briefing passed without incident to Trent Lott (Rep., Mississippi), the Senate majority leader, who supported the theme of Republican resolve with an unctuous grin assimilating both the promises of a television evangelist and the sympathies of a funeral director. His tan, like his smile, appeared to have been applied with a brush. He was a patient man, he said, and for three months he had been waiting for

President Clinton to send a budget to Congress—"a real budget, a budget that showed courage, showed leadership, that would preserve and protect Medicare, that would give some tax relief to working Americans. ..."

But the President had disappointed him, and so, alas, had the Democrats on Capitol Hill. Instead of sending a message of courage and leadership, they had sent a budget so extravagant in its expenditures that it was "all steak and Häagen-Dazs," not a real budget at all but a mess of partisan lies. The Republicans had given the Democrats their chance, but now they were "moving on," moving on if necessary to a budget of their own, "moving forward" to "a lot of good legislation that we can point to with pride."

So stirring were the senator's remarks that they prompted him to rise abruptly from his chair, undoubtedly in a hurry to cast a vote or write a law, and his sudden departure brought the press conference to an invigorating close before any churls hidden in the crush of reporters could ask questions likely to delay, even for an instant, the urgent tasks of renewal and reform. Nobody had the bad manners to ask about Dan Burton (Rep., Indiana), the congressman in charge of the committee directing the investigation of President Clinton's fund-raising methods who himself stood accused of extorting $5,000 in cash from a lobbyist representing the great and good people of Pakistan; neither did anybody say a word about Bud Shuster (Rep., Pennsylvania), the congressman in charge of the committee distributing $200 billion in highway money, who was conducting a romance with the principal lobbyist for the interests dependent upon his committee's largesse.

En route to the second news conference of the day, granted courtesy of Dick Armey, the House majority leader, who had acceded to the Republican limelight since the Speaker's January admonishment by the Ethics Committee, I congratulated one of the other reporters on the way in which the media performed a responsible public service by not pressing too hard on our harried politicians and thus protecting the American people against the deadly viruses of rage and alienation. In New York, I said, the press was often surly, failing to understand that rude questions slammed the doors of access, violated the rules of civility, offended the sensibilities of editors accustomed to walks in the White House Rose Garden.

Armey arrived forty-five minutes late, an affable man in an earnest suit who began by handing around a press release to the effect that the newly appointed poet laureate, a professor from Boston University by the name of Pinsky, had approved a policy of dispensing poetry to the general public at the nation's post offices.

On April 15 the government meant to supply copies of T. S. Eliot's "The Wasteland," which Armey thought a damn fine example of bureaucratic wit—"'April is the cruelest month' ... famous line ... and April 15, you see, is tax day ... cruel."

After making a few announcements about the legislation likely to appear on the calendar later in the week—two urgent bills, one of them denying food stamps to the inmates of federal prisons, the other refusing funding for assisted suicide—the majority leader invited questions, and in the terrible moment when a young reporter still in her fierce twenties mentioned the name of the lobbyist dallying with Congressman Shuster in an expensive townhouse on the Potomac River, I felt a tremor of alarm.

"Can you tell us something please," she said, "about Ann Eppard?"

Armey, God bless him, didn't show the least change of tone or expression. As amiable as tapioca and as innocent as a sunflower, he bestowed upon the company the bewildered smile of a country boy just off the bus from a depot sixty miles west of Waco, Texas.

"I'm sorry," he said, "I don't know who that person is."

I couldn't help but admire the majority leader's candor, and I remembered, sadly, how few of the important people in New York were brave enough to admit their own ignorance.

Q: "When will the Speaker pay his fine?"

A: "Ask the Speaker."

Q: "Why is the Congress repealing the Glass-Steagall Act?"

A: "The banking laws are very complex."

Q: "How does Congress intend to punish Mexico for its corrupt participation in the international drug trade?"

A: "We are very concerned about Mexico."

Q: "What about the Democrats who accuse the Speaker of malfeasance?"

A: "The pot can't call the kettle black."

Q: "When will the Republicans stop arguing among themselves?"

A: "Republicans are free and independent spirits. They march to their own drums."

Heartened by Armey's stolid and ox-like calm, I lingered in the halls to study the inspirational paintings—scenes of Columbus landing, the Pilgrims embarking, Cornwallis surrendering—and to wonder whether fifty years from now the guides would be pointing to the figure of Gingrich carved in Venetian marble. With any luck the schoolchildren might mistake him for Alexander Hamilton.

Flurries of tourists drifted through the halls like flocks of birds, their formations not unlike those of the Congressional Press Corps chasing the news from one whispering gallery to the next. From time to time important politicians appeared to scatter platitudes with the magnanimous aplomb of children throwing bread crumbs to the pigeons in the park. Senator Lott emerged from the Mansfield Room after a late lunch to say again that the Republicans were "moving on."

The afternoon debate in the Senate chamber consisted of three speeches about a bill directing the federal government to collect all of the country's nuclear waste and store it in the Nevada desert, at the site that already contains the remnants of the 800 nuclear-weapons tests conducted by the Defense Department over the last forty-odd years. Predictably, the two Democratic senators from Nevada (Harry Reid and Richard H. Bryan) thought the bill unwise, unnecessary, and unsafe. Arguing that the legislation served only the financial interest of the nuclear-power industry, they pointed out that it entailed the shipment of 85,000 metric tons of radioactive materials along highway and rail corridors in forty-three states—in canisters unable to withstand accidents occurring at speeds of more than thirty miles an hour. They might as well have been talking to the moon. As is usual in both the Senate and the House, the chamber was as bleakly vacant as an abandoned building in the South Bronx—a bored president pro tem presiding in the chair, two clerks, a stenographer, no more than forty tourists high up in the Visitor's Gallery (among them the platoon of Girl Scouts), and a single C-SPAN camera operating under remote control.

When the senators from Nevada finished saying what they had come to say, they collected their notes and shuffled quietly away. Some minutes later the sponsor of the bill, Senator Frank H. Murkowski (Rep., Alaska), entered through a door on the opposite side of the chamber and for the next two hours delivered an informative lecture about the glory of nuclear energy, the myopia of the Sierra Club, and the high-level radioactive-waste experiment that took place (safely and without unpleasant consequences) 1.8 million years ago in what is now the West African nation of Gabon. Inferring the experiment from a reading of the geological record, Murkowski said: "Mother Nature did it, and Mother Nature knows a hell of a lot more about nuclear fission than the Environmental Defense Fund."

Although possessed of little eloquence and no apparent humor, the senator doggedly recited every fact at his command, always willing to appreciate why his colleagues from Nevada might look upon 85,000 metric tons of nuclear waste as an unwelcome addition to their state. "Nobody wants the stuff," he said. "I can understand that. If it were not for Nevada, I'm sure it might be Vermont, where they have a lot of marble, or it might be Montana, where they have a lot of rock. But the point is it has to go somewhere. Somebody's got to take the stuff."

So also with politics, the waste product generated by the immense energy of the country's devotion to private and selfish enterprise. Somebody's got to take the stuff, and what better place for it than among the blocks of hortatory stone, some of them surprisingly lifelike, on Capitol Hill.

June 1997

Abracadabra

Who you gonna believe—me or your lying eyes?
—RICHARD PRYOR

On the final afternoon of this year's Masters golf tournament in Georgia, Fuzzy Zoeller, a prior winner of the event, attempted a joke about Tiger Woods, this year's winner, that fell, like a poorly played iron shot, into heavy sand. Woods at that moment was the best-known golfer in the country, famous not only for his exceptional talent but also for his young age (twenty-one) and his mixed race (part Asian, part black). On the assumption that Woods would have the honor of choosing what was to be served at the dinner preceding next year's tournament, Zoeller said he hoped the menu wouldn't consist of fried chicken and collard greens. It wasn't a good joke—obscure in its premise and tasteless in its point—but it was cast in the familiar, bantering tone (sometimes lighthearted, sometimes a little forced) popular in the multiracial company of professional athletes. The sportswriters on duty in the press gallery knew Zoeller as an amiable clown, loutish but well-intentioned, and the remark didn't arouse their political suspicions. None of them took note of it.

The television cameras were more literal-minded and less tolerant. Five days later CNN broadcast a clip of the clumsy witticism, instantly transforming Zoeller the bumbling jokester into Zoeller the Neanderthal bigot. High-minded newspaper columnists in New York and Washington handed down writs of summary judgment, and before the week was out Kmart, the retailer that employed Zoeller to endorse its golf equipment, deemed him no longer fit to be seen standing in the aisles of an outlet store with the lawn mowers, the suntan lotion, and the dog food.

Pursuant to the iron laws of wholesome cliché that govern the kingdom of big-time sports, Zoeller's punishment was neither cruel nor unusual. As long ago as 1988, CBS dismissed as one of its sportscasters the Las Vegas oddsmaker Jimmy the Greek for remarking on the physical differences between black men and white men, and as recently as last March the National Basketball Association levied fines on both John Calipari, the coach of the New York Nets—for characterizing a sportswriter as a "Mexican idiot"—and David Halberstam, a Miami Heat radio announcer—for drawing a parallel between modern basketball teams and Thomas Jefferson's gang of field slaves.

The masters of the nation's games obviously can't afford any smudging of preferred images, a practice that if allowed to proceed unchecked might depress ticket sales and confuse the bards at *Sports Illustrated.* They tend to make more abrupt decisions and inflict more severe penalties than their peers in the movie business and the publishing trades, but the fear of ill-groomed expression shows up in all sectors of the public conversation—in political debates careful to keep to the rules of "civility," in the universities bound by the codes of "political correctness" (as recommended both by the apostles of the multicultural left and the defenders of the Eurocentric right), in the corporate annual reports that conceal the mechanics of the business (often a matter of gutting the suckers like so many chickens) behind the lovingly illustrated displays of affection for all our wonderful friends and satisfied customers at play in the meadows of the global future.

As the regulation of offensive speech has become increasingly strict over the last ten or fifteen years, the list of proscribed words and phrases has become correspondingly long, and by the age of ten most true and loyal Americans learn that when in the company of strangers or a television camera, it is never wise to tell careless jokes, mention watermelons, or bring up questions of sexual preference. A motley quorum of designated humorists, among them Howard Stern and Dennis Rodman, retain the right to affront the society's delicacy of feeling, but everybody else does so at his or her peril. Dr. Joycelyn Elders was cashiered as surgeon general of the United States in December 1994 after she uttered the word "masturbation," and even so celebrated a newspaper columnist as Jimmy Breslin was sent home for two weeks (presumably to wash out his mouth with soap) after referring—in conversation, not in print—to a fellow reporter at *Newsday* as a "yellow cur."

Prior to Zoeller's blunder on the eighteenth green at Augusta National, I had thought our skittishness about language followed from our deference to money. Accustomed to the forms of speech that depend on the telling of more or less competent lies (construed as advertising slogans, legal briefs, political campaign promises, insurance policies, divorce agreements, tax returns), we take for granted the discounted prices paid for truth and unlicensed humor. Words move the merchandise, and when the important money in the room admits to a liking for carrots, the attending knights and squires begin to talk about Peter Rabbit and gardens in Connecticut. If over a period of time the practice of commercial dishonesty leads to the habit of intellectual dishonesty, well, that is one of the costs of doing business in a competitive world suddenly crowded with treacherous Arabs and unscrupulous Chinese.

But because most of the commentary about Zoeller's expulsion into the unsponsored wilderness made no distinction between the means of expression (what Zoeller said) and the acts of doing (the practice of racial discrimination in the United States), I wondered whether we might not have found an even more primitive use for language—words deployed not merely as sales pitch but also as exorcism and incantation, the higher orders of euphemism invested with the power to correct the condition that they seek to conceal. Silence all the Fuzzy Zoellers in the world apt to mention fried chicken in conjunction with the name of a black man, and the weight of racial injustice will lift and vanish from the earth with the mist rising through the Georgia pines.

The faith in supernatural words is marvelous to behold, and during the same few days that Zoeller figured briefly in the news a good many of the stories elsewhere in the papers offered further testimonies to the preference for magical thinking. On Capitol Hill an impressive number of Republican congressmen were holding stolidly to the belief that by their sustained and earnest repetition of the words "balanced budget" they could restore the American economy to a state of fiscal grace. Although not yet swinging incense pots or walking around in circles, they disdained to listen to people who pointed out that the arithmetic makes no sense, that a government forced to balance current revenues and expenditures would cease operations in a matter of weeks. Nor were they to be troubled with the nuisance of real numbers. What they apparently had in mind was the salvation of souls, and having defined debt as sin, they had gone forth in the conviction that the federal budget resembles the monthly checkbook kept by the upright father of an exemplary American family (two sons, two daughters, six Bibles) living on a picture-postcard farm (twelve cows, three cornfields, twenty-seven pigs) back home in nineteenth-century Indiana. The farm prospered and the sons grew up to be clergymen because the father never borrowed a dime. Let the federal government do likewise, and all the crooked tax deals in Washington will lift as gracefully from the earth as the white-winged waterbirds rising from the marshes of the Potomac.

President Clinton meanwhile was traveling in Mexico with the glorious news that the United States would continue to send large sums of money to that happy and prosperous democracy because Mexico, once again, had proved itself a staunch and worthy ally in the war against drugs. The President's reassuring words suppressed the less reassuring facts—e.g., that last February the commander of the Mexican antidrug forces, General Jesús Gutiérrez Rebollo, had been arrested for supplying information to one of the Mexican drug cartels; or that the cocaine shipments through Mexico from Peru to the American border provide at least $6 billion a year in bribes to favorably placed officials in the Mexican oligarchy. Why spoil a sunny afternoon in romantic old Mexico with dismal memories and melancholy doubts?

The front-page dispatch to the *New York Times* didn't list the names of the President's traveling companions, but Maureen Dowd mentioned the President's newly acquired friendship with Robert H. Schuller, pastor of the Crystal Cathedral in Orange County, California, and had the Reverend been present he no doubt would have helped everybody through what must have been a difficult day by reciting one of his cheerful slogans—"Turn your hurt into your halo," or, more triumphantly, "God plus me equals a majority."

As with the war on debt, the war on drugs is made of words, but then so was the Bre-X mine in Borneo, and while President Clinton was stopping the Mexican cocaine traffic with a force of heavily armed verbs, the holders of stock in Bre-X were trying to figure out what price they had paid for their faith in a magical noun. The newspapers offered different understandings of the larger lessons to be learned—how and why 200 million ounces of gold had vanished overnight—but on the outline of the story all the reports agreed:

A Canadian stock promoter by the name of David G. Walsh, a citified man who never once in his life had prospected for anything, not even for quartz or lead, ventured into the jungles of Borneo in 1993, and there, along the banks of Busang Creek, he discovered, much to his wonder and delight, the richest gold mine in the world. Although he was bankrupt at the time, and the stock in Bre-X, his exploration company, was trading on the Canadian stock exchange at two cents a share, the intrepid Walsh persevered, overcoming immense obstacles (fires, snakes, malaria, corrupt Indonesian mining officials), and was fortunate to engage the services of two clairvoyant geologists who knew how to divine the presence of precious metals in what they called "the footprints of volcanoes." For the better part of four years, Walsh and his geologists (Michael de Guzman and John Felderhof) drilled holes and collected core samples; they didn't mine gold in any commercial quantity, but their estimates of the worth and size of what they had found moved ever upward, from 30 million ounces to 40 million ounces, then to 70 million ounces, and lastly to 200 million ounces. The price of Bre-X stock rose on a parallel curve, from two cents a share to $50 a share to $200 a share. Content to believe Walsh's fantastic story, none of the buyers of the stock (among them mutual-fund managers for Fidelity Investments, Invesco, and American Express) sought to verify the geology. A lot of stockholders were making a lot of money, and why spoil a romantic interlude in the mysterious Orient with foolish questions and dismal facts?

But then, alas, it came time to prove the existence of the gold to somebody other than Walsh and his geologists, and so de Guzman was sent, presumably with a bag of first-class ore, to the mining company hired to operate the mine. Unfortunately, he fell out of the helicopter bringing him to the appointment (nobody yet knows why), and soon afterward the price of Bre-X shares on the Toronto Stock Exchange dropped at an equally sudden rate—$3 billion, or 80 percent of the company's value, in less than half an hour.

Trading in the stock had been suspended at $1.95 a share when President Clinton returned to Washington to find the Republican congressmen still murmuring the sacred budget chant and the Department of Health and Human Services busily at work on a similar ceremony involving sustained repetitions of the word "abstinence." The newly revised welfare laws allow the government to divide $250 million among those states and school districts that agree to indoctrinate their students with the belief that any and all sexual acts taking place outside the bonds of marriage were "likely to have harmful psychological and physical effects." The teaching was to be presented as a law of nature—repeated every day, no ambiguous exceptions to the rule, no loose talk about contraception, no alternative paths to virtue. A few of the state and school officials quoted in the papers thought that maybe the terms of the agreement were a trifle rigid, not to say narrow-minded and cruel, but among the nation's 16,000 school districts, 4,000 already provide an "abstinence only" curriculum, buttressed by educational videos in which, when a student asks, "What if I want to have sex before I get married?" the instructor replies, "Well, I guess you'll just have to be prepared to die. And you'll probably take with you your spouse and one or more of your children."

By the second week in May, the story of Zoeller's transgression had drifted over the horizon of the news with the stories about the fictitious budget and the nonexistent Mexican drug trade, and on a plane to Rome I could find nothing in the papers about the Reverend Schuller or the Bre-X mine.

But the line of thought that I'd been chasing for several days was implicit in the ruins of the old Roman empire, which gradually destroyed itself by substituting the faith in a legion of miraculous words for the strength of armies and the weight of walls. Walking one afternoon on the Palatine Hill among the broken stones that once burnished the glory of the Emperor Domitian, I knew that had I been present on that same height at the end of the first century A.D., I would have been slow to question the welcome lies told by Chaldean soothsayers or the masters of the Colosseum's gladiatorial shows. The world was Rome's toy, and who could doubt the immortality of the empire? The governors of distant provinces exacted tribute from the lesser peoples of the earth by means not unlike those of our own transnational corporations, and a favorite charioteer in the Circus Maximus earned as much from a day of successful racing as the winner of this year's Masters. The gentry on the Palatine Hill learned over time that humor was as dangerous a commodity as truth, and we can assume that the conversation was enlightened, tactful, well-groomed, in all ways politically and demographically correct. Domitian inclined to testiness, and he was in the habit of executing people who committed the crimes of offensive speech. Actors who made jokes as witless as Zoeller's were torn to pieces by dogs.

Standing on what little was left of a marble pavement that once supported a temple of Apollo, I couldn't remember which words the

Romans translated into wands and wishbones, but presumably they relied on a corollary faith in the first-century avatars of Deepak Chopra and the balanced budget.

July 1997

In the Garden of
Tabloid Delight

Caught in the relaxing interval between one moral code
and the next, an unmoored generation surrenders itself to
luxury, corruption, and a restless disorder of family and morals.
— WILL AND ARIEL DURANT

*T*he news media last May bloomed with so exuberant a profusion of sexual scandal that by the first week of summer it was hard to tell the difference between the front-page political reporting and the classified advertising placed by men seeking women and women seeking men. Every day for thirty days some sort of new or rare flowering appeared in the garden of tabloid delight, prompting the headline writers to dance joyously around the maypoles of 72-point type, singing their songs of spring with lyrics supplied by a grand jury or the police. Some of the stories were better than others, and although not all of them resulted in invitations to talk to Oprah, even a brief summary of the leading attractions fairly describes the gifts of the season's abundance.

MAY 2—Eddie Murphy, noted comedian and screen actor, found by sheriffs deputies, at 4:45 a.m. on Santa Monica Boulevard in West Hollywood, in the company of a transvestite prostitute.
MAY 10—Congressman Joseph P. Kennedy declines to explain how it came to pass that his younger brother Michael, thirty-nine, embarked

upon a love affair with the fourteen-year-old girl employed as the baby-sitter to his infant son.

MAY 20—Marv Albert, well-known television sportscaster, indicted in Virginia on charges of tearing at a woman's flesh with his teeth.

MAY 22—Frank Gifford, another famous television sportscaster, reported to have been photographed in a New York hotel room, parading around on a bed with a woman not his wife.

MAY 22—Lieutenant Kelly Flinn, "the perfect picture girl" of the United States Air Force and the first woman to command a B-52 bomber, drummed out of the service for committing adultery with a civilian soccer coach.

MAY 27—The Supreme Court directs the President of the United States to answer questions about the administration of his penis, all nine justices concurring in the opinion that the discussion cannot be postponed for reasons of state.

MAY 30—Staff Sergeant Vernell Robinson, Jr. is expelled from the United States Army and sentenced to six months in prison for forcing sodomy on five female recruits.

JUNE 2—Major General John E. Longhouser announces his retirement from the army and resigns his command of the Aberdeen Proving Ground (the scene of the crimes committed by Sergeant Robinson) because an anonymous tipster telephoned headquarters to report that five years ago, while briefly separated from his wife, the general had formed a liaison with a female civilian.

JUNE 3—Concerned Women for America characterizes lawyer Bennett's legal tactics as those "normally used by a rapist's attorney" and reminds him that two years ago President Clinton signed a law excusing sexually abused women from questions about their prior conduct.

JUNE 4 (late morning)—Lawyer Bennett disavows his proposed line of questioning and recommends the appointment of Air Force General Joseph Ralston as the next chairman of the Joint Chiefs of Staff, despite the general's confession that fourteen years ago (while separated from his wife) he carried on a love affair with a woman in the CIA. Secretary Cohen says that the time has come "to draw a line" against "the frenzy" of allegations spreading panic among military officers in all grades and ranks: "We need to come back to a rule of reason instead of a rule of thumb."

JUNE 6—The major news media, allied with indignant voices in both houses of Congress, overrule Secretary Cohen's call for reason. If bomber pilot Flinn must wear the scarlet letter, how then does fighter pilot Ralston escape the same marking?

JUNE 7—Congressman Kennedy informs 2,000 cheering delegates to the Democratic State Convention in Salem, Massachusetts, that he is "so very sorry, so very, very sorry" for any damage that his brother might have done to the baby-sitter or the baby-sitter's family.

JUNE 9—General Ralston withdraws his name from consideration as chairman of the Joint Chiefs of Staff.

The news offered so many occasions for pious or ribald commentary that any chance of agreement about what any of it meant was lost in a vast din of clucking and sniggering. The upscale newspapers published prim, op-ed-page sermonettes (about the country misplacing the hope chest filled with old family values); down-market talk-radio hosts told prurient jokes (about Paula's mouth, or Marv's toupee, or Bill's mole); the television anchorpersons were merely happy to be told that a lot of important people (many of them grown-ups and some of them celebrities) had been seen loitering (well past their bedtimes) on Love Street.

Although a few of the country's more high-minded commentators attempted professions of shock and alarm, the sentiments didn't draw much of a crowd. Most Americans know by now that the country's moral guidebooks (government-inspected, church-approved) fail to account for the political, economic, social, and technological changes that over the last 100 years have reconfigured not only the relation between the sexes but also the Christian definitions of right and wrong. The old guidebooks were written for nineteenth-century travelers apt to fall afoul of Satan in a San Francisco bordello, and either they require extensive revision or we need to adjust our present behavior. For the time being, the words don't match the deeds, and the ensuing confusion inflates the currencies of scandal. But because not enough people can agree to common terms of discourse, whether to begin with A for Abortion or with C for Clone, whether to proceed with reference to the Bible or to the *Kinsey Report,* we avoid the arguments by classifying human sexuality as a consumer product—a commodity, like cereal or furniture polish, packaged under as many brands and in as many forms (powdered or freeze-dried) as can be crowded onto the shelves in the supermarkets of desire. The commercial presentations allow us to have it both ways from the end and all ways from the middle—to meet the demand for hard-line feminist theory and the Victoria's Secret catalogue, for Robert Bork's sermons and Tony Kushner's plays, for breast or penile implants and software programs blocking out displays of nudity on the Internet, for as many different kinds of marriage (homosexual, heterosexual, open, closed, Christian, pagan, alternative, frankly perverse) as can meet with the approval of a landlord. The contradictions show up in every quarter of the society—posted on billboards and flashing on neon signs, available twenty-four hours a day on both the Playboy and the Disney channels, in the fashion photographs selling Donna Karan's dresses and Giorgio Armani's suits, in David Letterman's jokes and Senator Strom Thurmond's speeches, in the mirrors behind a hotel bar or on the walls of a health club, in the leaflets and lectures distributed (sometimes with condoms) to grammar school students, in newspaper ads hawking big-city prostitutes with the same adjectives that greengrocers assign to the grapefruit and the plums.

As might be expected of people engulfed in a haze of quasi-pornographic images, the subsequent confusion raises questions to which nobody has any good answers but which in the meantime provide the topics for the best-selling books of ethical self-help. What is moral, and where is virtue? Who is a man and who a woman, and how do I know the difference? Is marriage forever, or is it another one of those institutions (like the churches and the schools) wrecked on the reefs of progress? Do the doors of the future open only to people who observe the rules and watch their diets, or must we, as true Americans and therefore rebellious at birth, knock down the walls of social convention? Suppose for a moment that we wish to obey the rules: What do they mean and where are they written?

During the daylight hours such questions take the form of political disputes—about a woman's due or a man's debt, about the reasons why a gay and lesbian alliance is marching in Beverly Hills, about the academic poetess who didn't receive tenure, or the diaspora of Real American Men (hard-drinking and unshaven) tracking the spoor of William Faulkner's bear in a Mississippi forest. Like CNN or Batman, the questions never sleep, and late at night they turn inward and existential—am I inside the television set with Marv and Paula and Kathie Lee, or am I out here in the middle of nowhere with the wrong nail polish and last season's beer? Is the search for the perfect orgasm like the search for the perfect apartment—always lost and never found? If I highlight my hair and redistribute the weight of my stomach, will I live happily ever after in the land of Calvin Klein?

Maybe the questions need never be answered, but when and if we get around to doing so, we at least should admit that the events of the last fifty years can't be ignored or reversed. It's no good demanding (as do quite a few of our prophets on the Christian and neoconservative right) that the changes be sent back for credit to Bloomingdale's or L. L. Bean, or that somehow it still might be possible to bring back the summer of 1947. Most of the changes probably have been for the better rather than the worse. It's true that freedom doesn't come without its costs, but how many people willingly would return to a society that insisted upon the rigid suppressions of human sexuality dictated by a frightened aunt or a village scold? In 1947 a Hollywood movie couldn't be released to the public without the prior consent of the Hayes office, a bureau of censors loyal to the rules of decorum in effect at a New England school for girls. Husbands and wives couldn't be seen occupying the same bed, and children were brought into the world by storks. Under the threat of boycott by the Catholic Archdiocese of New York, Leo Durocher, the manager of the Brooklyn Dodgers, was suspended from the team during the 1947 season because he was conducting a love affair with Laraine Day, an actress to whom he was not married. The booksellers in Boston banned the sale of novels found guilty of sentences that described either the hero or heroine in states of wanton undress. Young men at college in 1947 hadn't been introduced to television, much less to Robert Mapplethorpe or Helmut Newton; genetics was a subject that had to do mostly with mice, a woman's place was in the home, and sex was something that happened in France.

Looking back on the transformations that have occurred within the span of my own lifetime, I remember that during the decade of the 1960s, in the early stages of what later became known as the sexual revolution, the photographs in Hugh Hefner's *Playboy* magazine opened a window in what I suddenly saw as a prison wall made of sermons in Protestant stone. I lose track of chronological sequence, but the rules seemed to change every year with the new fall clothes—first the forwardness of young women relieved of their inhibitions by the birth control pill, then the grievances (some of them surprising, most of them just) revealed in the commotion of the feminist movement, eventually the enlarged and public assertions of the gay and lesbian points of view, lastly the news that women no longer require men to perform the functions of husband and father. These days a woman of almost any age can choose to bear and raise a child under circumstances matched to her own history and understanding of the world—with a husband, with a man not her husband, from a zygote supplied by a sperm bank, by a fertilized egg borrowed from her daughter or mother, by adoption with a gay man, by adoption with a lesbian companion, by adoption with herself as the sole parent.

Nor have the changes been confined to what Pat Robertson likes to imagine as the red-light districts of Los Angeles and New York, as if the appetite for sexual fantasy presupposed a jaded, metropolitan taste. When the news of adultery usurped the headlines in late May, the *New York Times* dispatched a reporter to search the country for pockets of Christian rebuke. Generals were falling like nine pins into the gutters of lust, and the editors assumed that west of the Hudson somebody cared. The reporter, Carey Goldberg, returned with the news that not many did. A woman in Greenville, South Carolina, speaking on behalf of a clear majority, observed that although adultery wasn't legal in her state, "In this day and time, it's going on everywhere, and I mean everywhere." Were the authorities to enforce the law, she said, "everybody'd be in jail."

Among the guests who entertain Ricki Lake's afternoon television audiences with tales of their cross-dressing and cosmetic surgery, most of the people onstage come from places like Des Moines, Iowa, or Grand Rapids, Michigan. To meet the demand of the nation's video stores (most of them located in suburban shopping malls) the pornographic film industry last year provided 7,852 new releases (as opposed to the 471 supplied by Hollywood), and under the tolerant auspices of the World Wide Web, any child of nine sitting at a computer in Medford, Oregon, or Opa-Locka, Florida, can explore the landscape of sexual deviance first mapped by the Marquis de Sade.

About the perils of the voyage to paradise, the old moral guidebooks were not wrong. What at first glance looks like a ticket to the islands of bliss often proves more nearly to resemble a reserved seat in one of the eight dress circles of Dante's Inferno. I think of the numbers of people I've known over the last twenty or thirty years who sacrificed themselves on the altars of the imaginary self—marooned in a desolate marriage, so paralyzed by so many sexual options that nothing ever came of their talent and ambition, dead of AIDS at the age of thirty-one. The glittering invitations to everlasting orgy that decorate the drugstores and the movie screens are meant to be understood not as representations of reality but as symbols and allegories. Any customer so foolish as to mistake the commercial intent has failed to read properly the instructions on the label. One is supposed to look, not touch; to abandon oneself to one's desire not in a cocktail lounge but in a nearby mall.

The credit-card statements don't show the arithmetic of human suffering and unhappiness. It might well be true that if South Carolina enforced the laws against adultery, everybody would be in jail, but it is also true that sexual promiscuity and infidelity causes more misery (for the featured players as well as for the children in the supporting cast) than ever gets explained in the program notes. Over the years I've listened to a good many stories of bewilderment and loss, but none sadder than the one that appeared in the New York tabloids on June 9 about the eighteen-year-old girl, a student at the Lacey Township School in Ocean County, New Jersey, to whom a son was born at her graduation prom. During a break in the music, she left the ballroom, gave birth to the baby in a bathroom stall, wrapped it in paper towels, discarded it in a wastebasket, washed her hands, smoothed her evening dress, and returned for the next dance. From the perspective of the consumer market, the girl's actions make perfect sense. Sex is merchandising, and the product of desire, like Kleenex, is disposable. In the garden of tabloid delight, there is always a clean towel and another song.[1]

Like the high-speed computers that collate restaurant checks with telephone bills and drugstore receipts, the market can't tell the difference between adultery and a program of aerobic exercise; it doesn't know or care who said what to whom or whether the whip was meant to be used on a horse from Kentucky or a gentleman from Toledo.

Human beings who tailor themselves to the measures of the market

---

1 Babies dropped into garbage cans sometimes survive, but the one who died at the prom reminded me of another newspaper story I had read several weeks earlier about the Lacey Township School. The administrators apparently were worried about rumors of sexual malfeasance on the part of faculty or staff, and so they had ordered all adult personnel to approach the students with extreme caution. No touching, no hugs, no possibly suspicious pats on the shoulder, and when face to face with a student at a distance of less than three feet, the teachers and custodians were to raise both arms above their heads in a gesture of surrender. Both incidents (the one brutal, the other absurd) exemplify the character of what Will and Ariel Durant described as an "unmoored generation" drifting between one moral order and another.

float like numbers across the surface of the computer screen. Without the strength and frame of a moral order—some code or rule or custom that provides them with a way and a place to stand against the flood of their own incoherent desire—they too often lose the chance for love or meaning in their lives, unable or unwilling to locate the character of their own minds or build the shelters of their own happiness.

The loss of identity is good for business. The conditions of weight-lessness not only set up the demand for ballast heavier gold jewelry, more golf clubs, bigger cigars—but also encourage the free exchange of sexual identities, which, like the liquidity of cash, preserves the illusion of infinite options and holds out the ceaselessly renewable prospect of buying into a better deal. The pilgrims in search of a more attractive or plausible face can try on the 1,001 masks to which Freud gave the name of polymorphous perverse and to which the trendier fashion designers now affix the labels of androgynous chic. The structures of gender present themselves as so much troublesome baggage impeding the migration into F. Scott Fitzgerald's "orgiastic future." Let human sexuality be understood as a substance as pliable as modeling clay, and maybe it becomes an asset, easily worked into the shape of a stockmarket deal, a music video, a celebrity crime.

Transferred to what was once known as the public square, the descent into narcissism makes of politics a trivial pursuit. A society adjusted to the specifications of the tabloid press draws no invidious distinctions between the foreign and domestic policies of the President's penis and the threat of nuclear annihilation. Both stories guarantee record sales at the newsstands. On the day after the Supreme Court certified Paula's complaint about Bill (which also happened to be the day on which Boris Yeltsin announced at the NATO conference in Paris that Russia no longer would target its missiles on New York and Washington) the newspapers assigned the bigger headlines to the targeting error that either did or did not take place six years ago in an upstairs room of the Excelsior Hotel in Little Rock, Arkansas.

The distribution of news value should have come as no surprise. The voters last November saw in Clinton's narcissism a reflection of their own self-preoccupations and although well aware of his appetites for hard women and soft money, they were happy to send him to Washington as a representative of their collective moral confusion—a man no better than the other men that one was likely to meet at a sales conference or in a topless bar, always smiling and polite but in it for the money, in his own way as much of a hustler as Paula, as lost as most everybody else in the maze of amorphous sexuality. One day he appears in his masculine character (speaking sternly to the Serbs or the Albanians, making the strong, decisive, executive movements expected of a successful American businessman); the next day he shows up smiling like a debutante, pouring sentiment and sympathy into the teacups of the White House press corps, bravely holding back the tears that he otherwise would shed for a flood victim, a welfare mother, or a sick dog. Who but the old fools at the Pentagon could expect such a man to keep his penis in his pants or his fingers out of the Boston cream pie? The poor fellow is always so desperately needy, so insatiably eager for approval and affection, that it's a wonder he hasn't yet sold the Lincoln Memorial to a Korean amusement park.

A President so obviously unable or unwilling to tell the difference between right and wrong (much less, God forbid, to stand on or for anything other than the platform of his own need) clearly cannot ask anybody to grow up. He presents a role model not unlike that of Peter Pan (albeit an increasingly stout Peter Pan) and so excuses the rest of the class from the tedium of moral homework. With such a President, why bother to aspire to an adult code of ethics? We need not seek our own best selves, and in the meantime we inoculate ourselves against the viruses of age and idealism, which, as the advertising agencies well know, depress sales and sour the feasts of consumption.

Sex in the United States is no laughing matter, and although the commercial synthetics tend to leech the life out of the enterprise—the chance of meaning and the hope of intimacy as well as humor and eroticism—I take it for granted that the promises of eternal youth and everlasting orgy will continue to be more widely available and more innovatively sold. I'm glad that I'm not twenty years old, my name, address, and DNA stored in a data bank available to any mail-order operation. I expect that it probably would take me another twenty years to solve the riddle of my own identity, which is, of course, the point. If I knew who I was, why would I keep buying new brands of aftershave lotion, and how then would I add to the sum of the gross domestic product?

Given the sophistication of our current marketing techniques and the boundless resource of human curiosity and desire, the media undoubtedly will continue to post their scarlet letters and deliver their bouquets of scandal. The demand for gaudier sensations, for more telephone sex and brighter lip gloss, presumably will foster competing markets in small-time puritanism. Absent a unified field of moral law that commands a sufficiently large number of people to obedience and belief, with what else do we fill in the blanks except a lot of little rules—rules about how to address persons of differing colors or sexual orientation, about when to wear fur and when not to eat grapes, about what to read or where to smoke?

Although I can imagine books of rules as extensive as encyclopedias, I can't imagine them quieting the rage of the market. If I can lust after the girls on 300 pornographic cable channels, why can't I order one from a shopping network? Maybe the finer resort hotels will furnish their first-class suites with hospitable, omnisexual tennis pros in the same way that they place little squares of chocolate on the pillows. Who knows but that it might be possible to design one's children in the way that one decorates a house, choosing preferred characteristics (gray eyes, sixty-four teeth, strong backhand) from swatches of DNA instead of from bolts of fabric or chips of paint. If the editors of the *Globe* can pay an airline stewardess $75,000 to pose with Frank Gifford for the video camera in the Regency Hotel, what will they bid for the sight of a fireman in bed with Barbara Walters?

For the time being, and not yet having discovered a system of moral value that corresponds to the workings of big-time, postindustrial capitalism, where else can we live except in the garden of tabloid delight with Marv and Bill and Paula and Batman? Unless we wish to say that what is moral is what an insurance company will pay for (which, in our present circumstances, comes fairly close to the truth), what other arrangement meets the presumption—accepted as revered truth on both the liberal and conservative sides of the bed—that ethics and politics constitute increasingly marginal subsections of economics? If the lights must never go out and the music must always play, how do we even begin to talk about the discovery or construction of such a thing as a new moral order? Who has time for so slow a conversation? Who could hear what was being said?

August 1997

The Life

There are two things that are important
in politics. The first one is money, and I can't
remember what the second one is.

— MARK HANNA

Throughout the month of July the Senate Committee on Governmental Affairs conducted an investigation of the ways in which President Clinton raised money for last year's election campaign, and it was like listening to gardeners discuss the beauty of compost. Here at last was the most important subject in the world—loftier than budgets, grander than impeachments, more serious than bombs. For once the senators looked interested in the proceedings. What they were talking about was their lifework, their profession, their noble art, and they weren't about to be trifled with by mere pretenders and clumsy amateurs. Over the course of many years the sixteen members of the committee probably had collected an aggregate sum well in excess of $200 million for their own campaigns and those of their friends, and they knew all the moves—every nuance of obsequious gesture, every turn of wheedling phrase, which smiles were easy and which were not, when to sneer and how to crawl, whom to snub and what to kiss.

The rules of political fund-raising lately have become as complicated as the rules of etiquette that governed the comings and goings of Louis XIV's courtiers at the palace of Versailles, and while watching C-SPAN's montage of the testimony in the Hart Office Building I noticed that the committee's questions were better understood not as requests for information but as occasions for tart lectures in conduct and deportment. The witnesses were often awkward or nervous, below-stairs functionaries of little breeding and less taste whom one wouldn't hope to see standing around a punch bowl or a public trough. But the senators were upscale public servants, like French governesses or British butlers, and one knew that they could be counted upon never to confuse a Guatemalan valet with the ambassador from Egypt or Pakistan. They understood the fine distinctions between clean money and soiled money—between money that was as sweet as fresh milk and money gone sour in the sun, between money that could be followed and money that got lost in traffic, between companionable money and money that walked alone—and always it was instructive to listen to them display their knowledge of a subject to which they clearly gave their every waking thought. From their commentaries I learned what I'm sure will prove to be a useful set of lessons on that far-off, happy day when I hit the New York State lottery and can afford to buy a really expensive politician of my own.

On the first day of the hearing, members of the committee introduced themselves to the C-SPAN television audience with brief statements of uplifting principle. Something was wrong with the American system of government (too much money wandering around Washington off the leash of moral scruple), and the senators had come to set matters right, "searchers after truth" (Senator Joseph Lieberman, Dem., Conn.) seeking to address at this "historic moment" the questions of "our nation's basic sovereignty" (Senator Pete Domenici, Rep., New Mexico) in order to "enhance our government in the eyes of the American people at a time when our government sorely needs it" (Senator Fred Thompson, Rep., Tenn.) and so suppress the "desire to compromise the policy of the United States and to use money as a lever of power" (Senator Robert O. Torricelli, Dem., N.J.) by pledging "our lives, our fortunes and our sacred honor toward improving this democratic system for which so many young Americans have given their lives" (Senator Max Cleland, Dem., Georgia).

Every loyal and golden phrase deserving of a loyal and golden contribution, and all of them as finely shaped to their purpose as the instruments with which dentists draw teeth from widowers and shepherds wool from sheep. But as at any other fund-raising event, the senators were careful not to linger too long among the obligatory pleasantries, and after getting past the diversion of a sinister Chinese plot meant to sway last year's presidential election (the nominal pretext for the hearings but one for which nobody could offer any credible proof) they came at last to the subject dearest to their hearts—how to remove the stains from money that at first glance might seem too spoiled to be passed at the end of a pole to the fastidious consultants making the advertising buy at NBC or Disney. The proper procedures were more complicated than they looked, and in the 1996 election campaign President Clinton's fund-raising cadres—panic-stricken, desperate for cash, hounded by Dick Morris—had cut corners and made mistakes. Stupid mistakes. Careless and unnecessary mistakes. The kind of mistakes that that were likely to get everybody in trouble.

The tone of the questioning was impatient and exasperated. It wasn't that the senators objected to shaking down corporate lobbyists with threats of stringent regulatory legislation, or to selling high-quality "face time" at whatever price the market would bear (a practice that accounted for their presence in Washington), but there was a right way and a wrong way to do these things, and the Democrats had gotten out of hand. Out of hand and well beyond the bounds of propriety.

The first witness, Richard Sullivan, looked like a college cheerleader—thirty-three years old, handsome, likable, and genuinely confused. He had served as finance director to the Democratic National Committee during the hectic summer of 1996, and quite clearly he didn't know very much about steam-cleaning the dingier bundles of campaign money. His testimony took up the better part of three days, the committee gradually coming to regard him as "a good soldier" who had been led astray. Several senators took the trouble to intersperse their reprimands with helpful hints. Yes, it was perfectly appropriate to speak to foreign nationals (even to Chinese Indonesian billionaires) if the conversation took place on public television and one was wearing a suit from which all the pockets had been removed. But it was never correct to be seen alone at lunch with a foreign national among the ferns in the "infamous Four Seasons hotel." A well-bred finance chairman, whether Democrat or Republican, doesn't accept wire transfers directly from German or Chinese banks, but if the money is first sent to an American bank and there outfitted with a new checking account, a new name, and a hat from L. L. Bean, then even the most high-minded finance chairman can take it across K Street to meet Newt Gingrich or Vice President Gore. "Face-time" brings a higher price when sold as a boutique item, in very small quantities, to two or three contributors on golf carts.

Never give or take money on government property. Only louts blunder onto Air Force One or into the Library of Congress with a check or cash in hand. Say that I have $50,000 to spend, and that it is the President of the United Sates on whom I wish to make a favorable impression. First I attend the coffee ceremony in the Map Room of the White House, and there with maybe ten or twenty other guests I praise the coffee, listen to the President talk about Bosnia or poor people or his golf swing, eat no more than one Danish pastry, remark that the Map Room must have been a swell and exciting place in President Roosevelt's time (because he was using the maps to chart the course of World War II, praise the President (on any pretext that comes to mind), sip the coffee, compliment all the other people in the room (for their youth and vigor, never for their clothes or their jewels), inquire about the chance of rain, rise gracefully when a bell rings and the President is called away, praise the usher in the Marine uniform (not the steward in the white coat), walk proudly out of the building along the line of march indicated by the doorkeepers, praise the coffee once again (to anybody still within earshot), and so regain the anonymity of a common thoroughfare or public street. Then and only then is it permissible to write a check, which can be handed (in an envelope either blank or engraved) to a nearby aide-de-camp, who will carry it gingerly around the perimeter of the White House (being very, very careful not to step on the driveway or the lawn) to an office of the Democratic National Committee, where women in flowered dresses spray it with eau de cologne.

Similar courtesies and protocols must be observed when purchasing lesser politicians, among them all the senators on the committee, but circumstances vary, and the formalities occasionally can be abbreviated. Say that I happen to be riding in a car with a senator from Utah or a congressman from Texas, and that I wish to express my appreciation for his or her selfless and devoted service to the American people and/or an endangered rabbit. No coffee is at hand and no Map Room, but unless we happen to be driving through a military base or an Indian reservation, it is permissible to hand the check to the senator's assistant, even to stuff it into the assistant's pocket with a hearty laugh or a friendly nudge.

Sometimes a check must precede one's appearance at a dinner in the Library of Congress or the Museum of American History. The committee arranging the tables sends the bill in the form of an invitation, thoughtfully enclosing a schedule of fees matched to the available seating—$5,000 for a chair among the nonentities, $20,000 for a place on the dais, $50,000 for a photograph with the senator and his prize fish, $100,000 for everything on the list and a glass of champagne at the reception before the speech. The check need not be hand-delivered. The U.S. Postal Service doesn't come under the rule about government property, and if left to cure for three or four days in a worn canvas mailbag, the check loses the stench of a rich man's hand.

Clearly what troubled the committee, most especially the members of the Republican majority who had forced the holding of the inquiry, was not the question of reforming the campaign-finance laws (all agreeably ineffectual and none of which the senators sought to change or amend) but the far more important question of keeping up appearances. Some of the country's better-known politicians, among them President Clinton, had forgotten how to behave in polite company; they were slovenly and tactless and rude, and if they didn't improve their manners, the voters and taxpayers (that is, the common people for whom one must always set a good example) might form a poor impression of polities, even to the point of thinking, as Senator Cleland so forcibly reminded everybody, that "it's time to face the situation that we can place a 'For Sale' sign on both ends of Pennsylvania Avenue." A terrible thought, of course, un-American and coated with poisonous cynicism, but understandable in light of some of the news reports that had been seeping out of Washington like methane gas. Which was why Senator Don Nickles (Rep., Oklahoma) didn't think it was funny, not even the least bit amusing, when he showed Finance Director Sullivan a copy of the 1994 memorandum (from a special assistant to the general chairman of the DNC to an operative in the office of the White House deputy chief of staff) seeming to suggest that certain people in the Clinton Administration mistook a presidential election for a yard sale. The senator peevishly tapped his pencil while Finance Director Sullivan examined the document:

To: Ann Cahill
From: Martha Phipps
Re: White House Activities

In order to reach our very aggressive goal of $40 million this year, it would be very helpful if we could coordinate the following activities between the White House and the Democratic National Committee.

1. Two reserved seats on Air Force I and II trips
2. Six seats at all White House private dinners
3. Six to eight spots at all White House events (for example, Jazz Fest, Rose Garden ceremonies, official visits)
4. Invitations to participate in official delegation trips abroad
5. Better coordination on appointments to Boards and Commissions
6. White House mess privileges
7. White House residence visits and overnight stays
8. Guaranteed Kennedy Center tickets (at least one month in advance)
9. Six radio address spots
10. Photo opportunities with the principals
11. Two places per week at the Presidential CEO lunches
12. Phone time from the Vice President
13. Ten places per month at White House film showings
14. One lunch with Mack McLarty per month
15. One lunch with Ira Magaziner per month
16. One lunch with the First Lady per month
17. Use of the President's Box at the Warner Theater and at Wolf Trap
18. Ability to reserve time on the White House tennis courts
19. Meeting time with Vice President Gore

When Sullivan completed his review of the document, he looked up at the row of frowning senators with a puzzled smile, as if wondering what it was that he might have missed. He already had explained, at least five or six times, that the activities in question (among them the notorious "White House coffees" suspected of taking in $27 million) never were sold like football tickets; they were encouragements meant to "energize" prospective donors to the Democratic cause.

"Well?" said Senator Nickles.

"Well?" said Finance Director Sullivan, still unsure of the senator's point.

"So it was a pretty successful fund-raising effort?"

Sullivan's nervousness relaxed into a boyish grin. "It sure as hell was, Senator."

A brief splutter of laughter at the back of the room was quickly extinguished by the grim and bipartisan silence on the elected side of the microphones. As still as sixteen stones, the committee stared at Sullivan as if looking at a vulgar cousin to whom nobody could remember being related, and it was left to Senator Nickles to suppress the display of idle mirth:

"I am glad that some people think this is funny."

Which, at least from the committee's standpoint, it most certainly was not. Intent upon keeping up their own prices, the members had gone to a good deal of trouble to stage the hearing—at a cost of $4.3 million, $700,000 more than the White House spent entertaining its guests during the whole of President Clinton's first term—in order to prove (to the C-SPAN audience, to the editors of the *Washington Post,* to any corporation with a loose $250,000 to spend) that they retained their value as high-end merchandise. The market in politicians wasn't doing all that well lately, not when compared to the stock market or the $772,500 paid for President Kennedy's old golf clubs, and it surely would be a sad day in America—sad for its "searchers after truth," for its "basic sovereignty," for "the democratic system for which so many young Americans have given their lives"—when a fine-looking senator from Tennessee didn't fetch as handsome a price as a dress discarded by Princess Diana.

September 1997

Waiting for the Barbarians

The sunset colors of a civilization are the most lovely.
—JOHN STRACHEY

Always careless about keeping appointments, the barbarians tend to arrive a generation sooner than anybody expects, or six months after the emperor has fled. They accept the invitations of circumstance, and because they depend for their victories on the weakness enthroned within the city walls, it doesn't make much difference whether they come armed with spears or gatling guns. The empire collapses under the weight of its accumulated folly, its forum empty of politics, its orators as silent as the decorative marble, its principal citizens eager to buy the favor of a future with presents of amethysts and scrolls.

The spectacle was sufficiently familiar to the ancient Greeks that Aristotle accepted it as a proof of his hypothesis that the forms of government follow one another in a sequence as certain as the changing of the seasons—monarchy dissolving into despotism, despotism overthrown by democracy, democracy degenerating into anarchy, anarchy forcing the return of monarchy. He proceeded from the premise that all government, no matter what its name or form, incorporates the means by which the privileged few arrange the distribution of property and law to the less fortunate many. A government's longevity thus depends on the character of the oligarchy that supports its claims to legitimacy and pretensions to grandeur. But oligarchies bear an unhappy resemblance to cheese, and over time even the best of them turn rancid. The government might delay the procedure by making as difficult as possible the concentrations of wealth that inevitably fall to the lot of individuals equipped with financial talent, military genius or noble birth—but not even the strictest tax or sumptuary laws can nullify the logic of compound interest or postpone indefinitely the triumph of vanity. Sooner or later the men become pigs. An oligarchy that might once have aspired to an ideal of wisdom or virtue gradually acquires the character of what Aristotle likened to that of "the prosperous fool"—a man, or class of men, so bewildered by their faith in money that "they therefore imagine there is nothing it cannot buy." Once the oligarchy has been made stupid with insolence and greed, it's only a matter of time—maybe two or three decades, never more than three or four generations—before the government reformulates itself under a new row of statues and a new set of glorious truths.

Aristotle derived his understanding of politics from his study of Greek history in the fifth and fourth centuries B.C., which encompassed the rise and fall of the Periclean aristocracy, the democratic experiments (most of them failures) spawned by the catastrophe of the Peloponnesian War, and the long interval of petty tyrannies that preceded the conquest of Greece by the barbarians descending from the mountains of Macedon. Recurrent outbreaks of what the Greeks called *pleonexia* (the appetite for more of everything sold in the markets of desire—more houses, more dancing girls, more banquets, more prosperous fools) divided Athens into a city of the poor and a city of the rich, the one at war with the other and neither of them inclined to temper their bitterness in the interest of the common good. Aristotle mentions a faction of especially reactionary oligarchs who took the vow of selfishness by the swearing of a solemn oath: "I will be an adversary of the people [i.e., the commonwealth], and in the Council I will do it all the evil that I can."[1]

---

1 The oath might yet become mandatory among the more grasping Republican members of our own 105th Congress. Campaigning for reelection to the House of Representatives in the summer of 1996, Don Young (Rep., Alaska), chairman of the House Committee on Resources and an implacable opponent of the environmental cause, expressed a similar bias in an interview with Alaska Public Radio in which he described all environmentalists as "a socialist group of individuals that are the tool of the Democratic Party ... I am proud to say that they are my enemy. They are not Americans, never have been Americans, never will be Americans." Young's phrasing was

Aristotle's pupil, Alexander the Great, assembled a gaudy empire from the remnants of what was Periclean Greece, but it didn't long survive his own death in 323 B.C., and soon afterwards the turning of Aristotle's political seasons began to revolve around the horizon of Rome. The moral order of the Roman republic held together for 200 years, long enough to subdue the Carthaginians, punish Jugurtha and capture the Egyptian grain trade, but eventually it disintegrated in the chaos of civil wars (five in the space of twenty years), which exhausted the stores of political liberty and established the principle of despotism (sometimes benevolent, sometimes not) to which Caesar Augustus gave the name of empire.

Augustus took title to a Mediterranean world in which none of the thrones and dominions possessed the force, either of arms or of character, to sustain the risk of freedom. The cult of the individual replaced the collective ideal of the *polis;* the images of civic virtue dissolved into the mirrors of self-absorption, and in the hierarchy of popular esteem acrobats, cooks and astrologers occupied a higher rank than orators or magistrates. Reduced to selling the souvenirs of its once-upon-a-time glory, Athens had become a city famous for interior decorators of the soul (critics, philosophers, teachers of rhetoric), who furnished their conquerors with the ornaments of art and learning. At Antioch and Alexandria, as also at Ephesus and Pergamum, the reigning plutocrats imagined utopia as a suburban garden in which tame sophists came and went, talking of love potions and the lotteries of fate. All things private were to be preferred to all things public, and even second-class cities supported a multitude of statues (as many as 3,000 in the streets of Delphi and Rhodes) shaped to the specifications of wealthy individuals who ordered the precast torsos in one of four standard forms (all beautiful, all

---

intemperate, but among the great protectors of American oligarchy the sentiment is traditional. As long ago as 1887, explaining his veto of a bill meant to provide financial relief to the poor, President Grover Cleveland said, "The lesson should constantly be enforced that though the people support the government, the government should not support the people." Twenty years later, Arthur Hadley, the president of Yale, summed up the Orthodox Republican view in even more explicit language: "The fundamental division of powers in the Constitution of the United States is between the voters on the one hand and property owners on the other, the forces of democracy on the one side ... and the forces of property on the other side."

heroic) and then commissioned the sculptor to supply a handsome portrait of the missing head.

For another 200 years the more magnanimous of the early Roman emperors preserved the outward forms of the hollow republic, but after the death of Marcus Aurelius in 180 A.D., the *de jure* citizens had become so accustomed to their places as *de facto* subjects that the later emperors no longer maintained the shows of pointless debate about whether the laws were either important or just. Nor did they bother to write their own edicts or concern themselves with anything so boring as the administration of the state, and as the frontiers slowly collapsed under the press of barbarian invasion, a fatuous oligarchy discovered that it had forgotten the procedures for mounting a common defense. On the night of August 10, 410, when King Alaric's 100,000 Visigoths drove their bronze-headed battering rams through the walls of Rome, the emperor Honorius was in his palace on the Adriatic coast, arranging and rearranging his collection of prize poultry. Later the next day, while the Goths were busy looting the imperial city and murdering its inhabitants, a court chamberlain in Ravenna informed the emperor that Rome had perished. Honorius received the news with shock and disbelief. "Rome perished?" he said. "It is not an hour since she was feeding out of my hand."

The chamberlain explained that he referred to the city of Rome, not to the emperor's chicken of the same name. The clarification relieved the emperor of his anxiety. "But I thought, my friend," he said, "that you meant that I had lost my *bird*, Rome."

Not all the stories end with so absurd a moral, but over the last sixteen centuries the fall of empires and the ruin of nation-states invariably have been preceded by a comparable lack of attention on the part of the authorities nominally sovereign. A succession of Catholic popes in the late Renaissance preferred the adoration of their mistresses to the contemplation of the saints, and the rapacity of their political ambitions so degraded the image of the church that it was sapped of the strength to excommunicate the Protestant Reformation. The ruling aristocracy in late-eighteenth-century England couldn't conceive the possibility of losing a war with the American colonies. Enthralled by the dream of omnipotence, the ministers and peers responsible for the management of American affairs didn't think it worth their trouble to cross the Atlantic to see what it was they were talking about. Edmund Burke attributed their foolishness to "plentiful fortunes, assured rank and quiet homes."

Louis XVI devoted himself to the collecting of clocks instead of pullets, meanwhile surrounding himself at Versailles with a comforting swarm of courtiers amused by the satires of Voltaire and the romances of Rousseau and never once imagining that anything could go wrong with the potted orange trees. At St. Petersburg nearly 100 years later, Czar Nicholas II, Emperor and autocrat of all the Russias, placed on his head a heavy gold crown surmounted with a cross of diamonds, heartened by the pleasing prospect of an always bountiful future equipped with seven palaces, 15,000 court officials and 226 dancers in the Imperial Ballet. Speaking on behalf of the German plutocracy in 1933, and by way of reassuring a nervous steel magnate that in the Nazi Party big money had found its champion and savior, Fritz von Papen said of Adolf Hitler's election to the office of Chancellor, "We have hired him ... we have him framed in."

The prosperous fool is a familiar figure on the world political stage—a stock character like Harlequin and Pantalone in the old *Commedia del Arte*—and although I don't wish to suggest too close a parallel between Alan Greenspan and Marie Antoinette or between Barbara Walters and the emperor Commodus, I think it fair to say that after two centuries of experiment with the theory of the Enlightenment and the volatile substances of democracy, our own American oligarchy has grown tired of politics and bored with public speaking. Like the ancient Greek plutocrats among whom Aristotle noticed the marks of glittering stupidity, their contemporary heirs and assigns have persuaded themselves that "there is nothing that money can't buy," a revelation they regard as Heaven-sent and one from which they proceed to the assumption that now that capitalism has triumphed over every other ism that anyone can think of (liberalism and irredentism as well as communism and socialism) all the old political disputes amount to little more than a list of possible titles for next season's hit musical. Grateful for Francis Fukuyama's assurance that they have come safely to the end of history, America's ruling and possessing classes conclude that nothing remains to be done except the chores of maintenance—managing the distribution of the world's goods and peoples along the lines set forth in a strategic marketing plan, imposing the rules of a Victorian boarding school on the misguided thugs and bullies in the Southern latitudes who still think that something good can come from playing with explosives. The apostles of the global economy never tire of professing their belief in the divine mystery of the free market, offering as proofs of its benevolence the litany of always larger numbers—more office towers, better telephones, higher stock markets, greater rates of consumption and production, all fortunes rising on an incoming tide of prosperity. The transnational economic order inherits the ecumenical place once occupied by the Catholic Church, and the world divides, unevenly but along only one frontier, between Aristotle's cities of the rich and provinces of the poor.

The historians of the early Roman empire speak of "an Epicurean generation," myopic and selfish, devoted to the cults of celebrity, preoccupied with the pleasures of the bedchamber and the banquet table, excusing itself from the tedium of public affairs on the ground that politics, like the children and the laundry, were best left to the hired help. The description fits our own Epicurean generation, maybe not as literate as the one resident at Capua in the first century A.D. but vastly enlarged by the extensions of consumer credit and the science of telemarketing. Throughout the whole of the society plutocrats of all denominations and degrees (established, well-off, expectant, rich, aspiring, marginal, seriously rich) bow before displays of conspicuous consumption as if before special guest appearances by the great god Pan. The net worth of the shares sold on the New York Stock Exchange moves steadily upwards, posting a 50 percent gain over the last four years that constitutes the largest increase of sudden fortune ($4.1 trillion) known to the history of mankind. The managers of the country's enterprises ally themselves with anybody or anything that can turn a profit—with Snoop Doggy Dog and the pornographic film industry, with the drug and weapons trades, with Chinese merchants selling human organs extracted from felons sent to their executions on a schedule convenient to the demands of the market for a fresh liver or a tender heart. Senior officers of the *Fortune* 500 companies award themselves salaries of $2 million, $4 million, $10 million per annum and within the honeycomb of all large-scale American corporations the average ratio between the money earned by the costliest executive and the cheapest clerk now stands at 186 to 1. Summer houses at Southhampton rent for $125,000 a month; at upscale New York delicatessens ham sandwiches sell for $12, and across the broad expanse of America the Beautiful the nation's busiest and best-paid architects concentrate their efforts on the building of gambling casinos, golf courses and prisons.

The worship of money has taken its customary toll, and what we have in the United States at the moment is an oligarchy that confuses history with a board game like Monopoly or Chinese checkers, thinks that the future can be made to fit an ideological blueprint (supplied by The Heritage Foundation or The Friends of Newt Gingrich) and imagines that it can buy (for six points up front or a percentage of the gross) its escape from the wreck of time. The corollary descents into narcissism can be measured by almost any gauge that anybody cares to mention—by the privatization of the police forces as well as the public schools, or by the number of Academy Awards bestowed last April on a movie as solipsistic as *The English Patient*—but whether counted out in cash or marriage licenses or hogsheads of French cologne, the weight and sum of instant gratification shifts the balance of the common interest from the public square of politics to the private gardens of the self. In the old Roman republic (as again in the early years of the American experiment with constitutional government) respect, admiration and sometimes fame followed upon a career dedicated to the service of the state. The currencies of honor lost their value under the rule of empire, and the energies once drawn to the care of the *res publica* dwindled into the ashes of ceremonial sham. Alexander Hamilton advanced the idea of a government conducted by a disinterested class of patrician landholders—that is, by men already possessed of wealth and rank and therefore presumably relieved of the necessity to lie and cheat and steal. The proposition didn't sit well with the expectant capitalists who allied their ambitions and what little was left of their sacred honor with the commercial promise of what came to be known as Jacksonian democracy. After the Civil War the sons and heirs of well-to-do American families shunned the political stage on which "saloon keepers and horse car conductors" courted, in Henry Adams's phrase, "the cheers of an Irish mob."

As it was among the wealthy Romans in the second century A.D.—retired whenever possible to their villas by the sea, safely out of the emperor's sight and writing wistful letters to one another about the loss of ancient virtue—so also it is now with the wealthy Americans gone off to Florida or Connecticut, hidden behind stucco walls and tinted glass, exchanging rumors of liberal conspiracy, comforted by the wisdom of William F. Buckley, Jr. and Deepak Chopra, entrusting their hope of immortality to the photographers of *Fortune* and *Vanity Fair* rather than to the sculptors of marble portrait busts.

The retreat from the public forum lately has become a rout, effective at all ranks of the plutocracy and expressed not only as contempt for the government at Washington but also as a general loss of faith in the national institutions, among them the law courts, the hospitals, the press and the universities, that once embodied the highest ambition of the American democracy. The public opinion polls report a clear majority of respondents convinced that the brutalized forms of public life in the United States no longer can accommodate the promises of decency, freedom or justice. The findings reflect the recognition that under the aegis of late-twentieth-century capitalism it is the transnational corporation, not the church or the state, that bestows the gifts of meaning and purpose as well as the salvation of medical insurance, golf-club membership, pension and foreign travel. The locus of effective decision shifts to the smaller and more coherent concentrations of economic interest and intellectual force—to IBM and Mitsubishi, to mercantile city-states (among them Singapore and Orange County, California), to militant causes (in Israel or Iran or Northern Ireland), to political entities centered on a river valley or a conjunction of textile mills, to the judgment of armed bandits posted on the roads west and north of Sarajevo. Five hundred corporations control 70 percent of the world's trade, and conduct their own foreign policy; their servants and employees, often as numerous as the populations of thirteenth-century Florence or sixteenth-century London, pledge allegiance not to the American flag and the republic for which it supposedly stands but to Citibank or the Disney Company. National identity becomes a sentimental novelty, comparable to a picturesque background for a trendy movie or an important bar, and the American Congress and the American President serve at the pleasure of the commercial overlords on whose behalf the several divisions of government, like medieval bailiffs, collect taxes in the form of handsome subsidies and congenial interest rates.[2]

Expressed as popular entertainment, the generally low opinion of

---

2 Similar feudal understandings govern the administration of the NAFTA and GATT agreements. At the World Bank or the International Monetary Fund the power of decision rests with relatively few people who confer behind closed doors to fix the prices of silk and wine, linseed oil and wheat. The European Community makes no secret of its resemblance to a medieval guild. The sixteen unelected members of the directorate formulate the rates of exchange (for goods as well as currencies) that affect the lives of 340 million people in Europe, and the elected European Parliament that sits in Strasbourg serves without authority to make or unmake the laws, as an ornamental chorus meant to sing the empty praises of democracy.

government and all its works provides the agenda for the right-wing radio talk shows, advances the plot in countless movies and television dramas that exhibit the President of the United States as a hapless imbecile or criminal psychopath, boosts the sales of novels along the lines of Joe Klein's *Primary Colors* and Tom Clancy's *Executive Orders*. Both books headed the best-seller lists during the 1996 election year, the former a portrait of the Clinton White House furnished with the characters and attitudes believed to have been sitting around in the parlor of a nineteenth-century bordello on the Arkansas frontier, the latter proceeding from the premise that foreign terrorists had hijacked a Japan Airlines 747, which they then crashed into the Capitol dome, killing the President and most everybody in the Cabinet, hundreds of members of Congress, the Joint Chiefs of Staff and all nine Justices of the Supreme Court. That same summer the movie *Independence Day* exceeded all previous box office records with a scenario that inflicted an equally satisfying degree of damage on Washington, and a journalist named John Jackley published *Below the Beltway,* a book presented as nonfiction that depicted the city as a moral and intellectual swamp. Endorsing sentiments similar to those that inspired Timothy McVeigh to blow up the Murrah Federal Building in Oklahoma City, Jackley stipulated his loathing and visceral hatred for Washington, most especially its privileged classes ("the socialites, the politicians and the pontificators") and concluded his tour of the capitol with a word of warning: "So look out Washington ... because the peasants with their torches and pitchforks are gathering around the gates ... the smell of blood is in the air, and it isn't theirs."

Although I can understand why people outside the gates might rejoice in the slogans of revolt, I find it less comprehensible when the people inside the palace dress themselves up in similar attitudes of resentment and rage. And yet it is precisely those people who profit most handsomely from the government's guarantees who complain most loudly about the government being sworn to the service of Satan. For the last twenty years the Republican Party has campaigned on its collective promise to sweep the stench of politics from the streets of Washington. Politicians of both parties, even politicians as loyal to the status quo as Senator Robert Dole, stand for election and re-election in the pose of the noble outlaw come to dismantle "the system" invariably described as incompetent and corrupt. George Pataki, the governor of New York, mocks the administration of the state's criminal laws as "junk justice" and proposes legislation allowing prosecutors to appeal judicial rulings that contradict their own notions of sentencing and bail—thereby granting to a district attorney in Albany or Brooklyn or Saratoga the powers of summary judgment assumed by Clint Eastwood in *High Plains Drifter*. The House Majority Whip, Tom DeLay (Rep., Texas), declares that the federal judiciary "has run amok" and urges Congress to consider impeaching judges whose decisions run counter to his own definitions (presumably God-given) of right and wrong.

Only a truly stupid oligarchy could mount an attack on the institutions of government that provide it with the warrants of protection and the gifts of privilege. Who else but the government supplies the tax exemptions and the highway contracts? If not the government, who rescued the monied classes from the pits of bankruptcy when the prices on the New York Stock Exchange abruptly lost $479 billion of their value on October 19, 1987? Who pays the cost of rebuilding after floods in the Dakotas and hurricanes in Florida? Or defends the plutocracy against a siege of anarchy and angry mobs?

Because the private interest precedes the public interest, politicians who find politics beneath their dignity flounce out of Washington in a flurry of press releases proclaiming their refinement of feeling. Before the general election last November, fifty-three senior members of Congress—15 senators and thirty-eight congressmen—announced their decisions not to run for reasons of conscience or inconvenience: because the press was uncivil, because they were sick of begging money from their corporate patrons, because they were tired of telling lies. Why squander one's energies and good name on the writing of laws that nobody reads (much less understands or obeys) while it was still possible to pursue the far more important business of taking care of oneself? During the course of the presidential campaign, candidate Dole assured his audiences that if he lost the election he would return to his little house on the Kansas prairie, there presumably to read Cicero's speeches and contribute the occasional word of advice to those of his former colleagues still engaged in the work of government. Dole dropped the pretense on the day after the election. Instead of going home to Kansas, he accepted a partnership in one of the Washington law firms representing the tobacco industry, at the same time agreeing to appear as a television pitchman (for a credit card company) under the label of "Honest Bob." Susan Molinari (Rep., N.Y.), last year's keynote speaker at the Republican convention in San Diego, won re-election to Congress, but then, six months later, resigned the office to join former Senator Bill Bradley and former White House counselor George Stephanopoulos in the sandbox of network television.

Further testimonies to the diminishing interest in the *res publica* show up in every edition of the morning and afternoon papers—stories about this or that government functionary betraying the confidences of office in return for a book or a television deal, stories about Republican congressmen subtracting funds from scholarly projects meant to preserve and document the country's political history, stories about military officers dedicating their careers to the service of Venus instead of Mars.[3]

But among the myriad indices of the general loss of faith in government, probably the most vivid is the figure of the President. The voters last November knew that Clinton was caught in the nets of at least three examinations of his sexual and financial conduct, all of which he was likely to fail, but they also knew that he was a man so lacking in character that he couldn't ask any questions—at least not with a straight face—that might require his fellow citizens to correct their own weaknesses or temper their own appetites for self-love. His presence in the White House confirms the capitalist presumption—dear to the hearts of the people who paid for his election—that politics don't count for much in a world geared to the interests of the transnational economic order. If Clinton can be President, then clearly the office isn't worth the having.

---

3 The newspapers in the spring of 1997 brought word of three admirals and as many generals, one of them a prospective chairman of the Joint Chiefs of Staff, reduced in rank or drummed out of the service on the suspicion of adultery. But the story that produced the biggest headlines was the one about Lieutenant Kelly Flinn, a bomber pilot discharged from the Air Force for having carried on a romance with a civilian soccer coach. The lieutenant's defenders, among them the editorial page of the *New York Times,* thought the punishment as unfair as it was behind the trend of the times. In the world after the end of history, nobody expects the United States to wage a serious war, and Lieutenant Flinn enlisted in a military service that sells itself as a co-educational summer camp so attuned to the theme of personal development that it invites prospective recruits to "Be All You Can Be," to come and float "on airy thoroughfares" of the sky among "cloud puff-balls, torn, tuft-tossed pillows." Assume that the advertisements mean what they say—just like the ones about the athletic prowess inherent in Nike tennis sneakers and the gifts of intelligence that come with every cellular phone—and who could not forgive Lieutenant Flinn for thinking that as between the private and the public self, the larger realm of meaning was to be found among the tuft-tossed pillows of the former rather than the treacherous wind shears of the latter.

Like most everybody else who follows the story of American politics, my information is anecdotal and incomplete, and I have no idea how our opulent plutocracies will manage their passage into the next century. I read in the paper that the country spends $2 billion a year on the purchase of golf equipment (just the clubs and balls, not the shirts, the hats and the shoes), and I know that I live in a society rich beyond the Emperor Nero's dreams of avarice. But then, in the same paper, I come across the news that 21 million American families subsist on annual incomes of less than $25,000 (scarcely enough to pay a year's caddie fees at Pebble Beach), and I remember what happens to societies that allow the opening of too broad a gulf between Aristotle's cities of the rich and poor. That gulf is now greater than at any time since the heyday of Imperial Rome, but the oligarchy that presides over the administration of what was once the American republic finds no cause for alarm. To the contrary. Instead of attempting a more equitable division of the nation's wealth, the oligarchy seeks its greater concentration in monopolies always more narrowly held and implacably defended.

In June of this year both houses of Congress passed budget bills awarding 65 percent of a projected tax reduction to the richest 20 percent of the citizenry, while providing only 13 percent of the benefits to the poorest 60 percent. The numbers square with the attitudes of entrenched selfishness that have dictated government policy for the last ten or twenty years—the bias expressed as legislation that favors the merger of large corporations into even larger corporations (ABC with Disney, Boeing with McDonnell Douglas, Morgan Stanley with Dean Witter, etc.), curtails or eliminates the funds available to public education, encourages the systematic exploitation of the poor (most savagely by the HMOs and the insurance companies), deregulates the banking system, denies the possibility of complaint or redress on the part of common folk robbed by their feudal overlords. The last named bill, passed in June 1995, allows corporate officials (mutual funds salesmen, company presidents) to defend themselves against charges of fraud merely by saying that they genuinely forgot to disclose matters of pertinent fact—either because they were distracted at the time by more urgent concerns (a difficult bunker shot, something wrong in the engine of the Lexus) or because the thought of disclosure never crossed their minds.

As might be expected, the shining face of the global economy wears its brightest smile in the show windows of the media owned and operated by the same oligarchy that owns and operates the banks. The accompanying press releases predict limitless good news in a world joyfully blessed by open markets, convertible currencies and free trade. The financial magazines make no attempt to quiet their emotions or restrain the breathless tenor of their prose. Behold, men of genius and resolve—Billionaires! Visionaries! Entrepreneurs!—trading cable systems for telephone lines, and telephone lines for movie studios, and movie studios for cable systems, buying and selling the wells of celebrity that water the gardens of paradise.

I don't doubt that the comforts of the global economy are many and wonderful to behold. But they come at a cost that can be expressed in other sets of always larger numbers—the ones about the destruction of the forests and the fish, about the fast-rising slums that engulf the cities of steel and glass, about the dissolution of the ozone layer and the proliferation of sewer rats and nuclear weapons. The rule of law meanwhile loses its hold on the ferocious elites (corporate and predatory, often criminal) that with the force and arrogance of capital intimidate the world's parliaments (in China and Mexico, in Russia and Brazil as well as in the United States) in a manner not unlike that of the military commanders in the first century B.C. who bullied the Roman Senate with the force of arms.

Our American political classes in the meantime, being themselves complicit in the well-financed banditry at large in the world, paper over their superfluousness with gossip about Hillary Clinton's astrologer and the sins of children's television, about the wickedness of the National Arts Endowment and Gore's acquaintance among Buddhist nuns. Their insouciance unnerves me because I would have thought that the barbarism implicit in the restless energies of big-time, global capitalism requires some sort of check or balance, if not by a spiritual doctrine or impulse, then by a lively interest in (or practice of) democratic government.

The collapse of communism at the end of the Cold War removed from the world's political theater the last pretense of a principled opposition to the rule of money, and the pages of history suggest that oligarchy unhindered by conscience or common sense seldom takes much of an interest in the cause of civil liberty. Historical analogies deserve to be regarded with suspicion, and maybe it isn't necessary for the beneficiaries of a rich economy to trouble themselves with the chores of government; maybe (as per the editorials in the *Wall Street Journal,* and the endings of Arnold Schwarzenegger movies) all is for the best in this best of all possible worlds. The Byzantine Empire lasted for nearly 1,000 years, content with its genius for bureaucracy, dress design, church liturgy and political assassination.

At the G-7 Summit Conference held in Denver in June 1997, President Clinton's boast to the assembled heads of state ("America's economy is the healthiest in a generation and the strongest in the world") was neither idle nor false. The standard sets of statistics support the projections of boundless profit—low rates of inflation and unemployment, business booming, the Dow Jones Industrial Average approaching 8,000, more people buying golf balls and boats, large crowds pushing through the turnstiles at Disneyland and the Las Vegas casinos. At no point on the American compass do any of the nation's soothsayers discern even the faint stirrings of a rebellious wind. The slack-jawed heirs to the Kennedy name and fortune might ape the dissolute manner of the younger Roman dynasts who rallied to the cause of Cataline's conspiracy, but no tyrant comparable to Sulla or Pompey the Great threatens to arouse the populace to slaughter. No Robespierre has appeared in the balcony of the New York club scene, and although the American people have in large part indentured themselves to the corporations, they cannot be fairly described, at least not yet, as slaves.

Why then do I keep thinking of Aristotle's political seasons, or of Cavafy's consuls and praetors, "carrying elegant canes beautifully worked in silver and gold?" Possibly because when I listen to another futile speech by Madeleine Albright, or read the newest press release promoting the moral beauty of the stock market, I wonder how a society can long endure by defining truth as the acceptance of untruth, or by passing laws incapable of being enforced, or by thinking that freedom is a trust fund inherited at birth and certain to last a lifetime, or by saying, with Senator Alfonse D'Amato, that Americans deserve—as a natural right—permanent exemption from the indignity of terrorist attack. Watching July's Senate hearings on the topic of campaign finance reform (a discussion rendered useless by the committee's determination to conceal from itself the answers to its own questions), I thought of the historian Sallust remarking on the fecklessness of the decadent Roman republic that reduced the rule of law to a flourish of pompous rhetoric. Sallust's description of Rome in 80 B.C.—a government controlled by wealth, a ruling-class numb to the repetitions of political scandal, a public diverted by chariot races and gladiatorial shows—stands as a fair summary of some of our own circumstances, but as premonition it is surpassed by the remarks of the bookseller Rualt, writing to his brother from Paris in the summer of 1786:

> Money there must be, and there's an end to it; money for expenditure known and unknown; money for the ordinary and for the extraordinary; money for the five or six kings reigning in France who dip so generously into the public treasury; money for the king of Paris, the king of finance, the king of war, the king of the fleet, the king of foreign affairs, and the King of all these kings, who, they say, would be the thriftiest of them all if it weren't for his wife, his brothers, his cousins and so forth ...

> Finance has grown so powerful, so proud, so despotic that one must believe it can go no higher and must infallibly perish before many years have passed. When finance is honored, says Montesquieu, the state is lost. A fearful revolution is very imminent; we are very, very close to it, at any minute we are going to reach a violent crisis. Things cannot go on longer as they have been, that is self-evident. There is nothing but speculation, finance, banking, discount, borrowing, wagering, and payment. Every head is glued to money, crazy with speculation. A little patience, and we may see some pretty goings-on in 1800!

Until the last appalling moment when the barbarians come clattering through the gates mounted on Mongol horses or German tanks, nobody in the imperial city ever imagines the scenes of destruction as anything other than illustrations in somebody else's history book. Cavafy wrote his poem in 1898, but he was an obscure Greek living in Egypt, and what did an obscure Greek have to say to the wits and crowned heads of Europe, or to the scientists and duchesses and top-hatted statesmen celebrating, with champagne and portraits by John Singer Sargent, the triumphant finale of what Barbara Tuchman in *The Proud Tower* characterized as "the most hope-filled, change-filled, progressive, busiest and richest century the world had ever known." Great Britain stood at the zenith of empire, its self-assurance exactly phrased by a leading Tory editor of the day (Alfred Austin of *The National Review*) who, on being asked by Lady Paget and Lady Windsor to tell his idea of heaven, paused for only the briefest of moments before saying that he desired to sit in a garden and receive a flow of telegrams announcing alternately a British victory by sea and a British victory by land; Germany was entranced by the music of Richard Strauss, also by Kaiser Wilhelm's wardrobe of military uniforms and Nietzsche's dream of the *Ubermensch;* America had just won a splendid little war with Spain, and Colonel Teddy Roosevelt, the hero of San Juan Hill, was blowing the bugles of Manifest Destiny at "the ignorant and inferior races" in Panama and Manila Bay; the French were briefly distracted by the Dreyfus Affair, but not to the point of forgetting that their civilization was immortal; in Russia all the best people were reading *The Future of War* (six volumes of iron-clad prose written by a complacent railroad magnate named Ivan Bloch) that had become the rage in Moscow and St. Petersburg with its incontrovertible proofs—financial, social, cultural, political and historical proofs, all of them buttressed by graphs and charts—promoting the assertion that the latest industrial and scientific advances had obviated the need for war, that war was purposeless and obsolete, a ridiculous and antiquated pastime likely to have as little place in the twentieth century as Napoleon's merry-go-round horses or Nelson's toy fleet.

The guests taking their turns at the waltz in the ballrooms of the *belle epoque* wouldn't have known where to look on a map for the names of the towns on the Western Front—Passchendaele, Ypres, Cambrai, Château-Thierry, Verdun—soon to become synonymous with the end of what was once a world. One hundred years later I can no more guess at the sequence of events lying below the horizon of a new century than could the Duke of Devonshire or the Czar of All the Russias, but I think it probable that the United States will find it increasingly difficult as well as irritating and unnecessary to sustain the risks of freedom. The trend of the times favors the rule of force (more laws restricting the liberty of persons, fewer laws restraining the rights of property), and the locus of the hope for a brighter future or a better life shifts from the politics of here and now to the lotteries of there and then. If our legislators no longer write their own laws, or our merchant princes their own press releases and our university presidents their own commencement speeches, then who rises to the defense of liberty? An oligarchy that reads from rented scripts already has put itself up for sale. The transfers of title to the new owners of state don't always entail the massacre of the former occupants. Sometimes the barbarians amuse themselves by trying on the costumes of civilization (Cavafy's crowns and the scarlet togas); a good deal of real estate changes hands, but after a few years the department stores reopen, a new gallery of faces makes itself known to the gossip columnists on duty in the best restaurants and the better hotels, and nobody who is still somebody can remember when or why it was that they didn't think that tyranny was exciting and glamorous and fun.

September 1997

Index